Wisdom
Builds

Huldah Dauid

The Awakening Remnant Koalition
California

Contents

This book is dedicated to every woman, who at one time or another, expressed the willingness to build her "house", but lacked the necessary tools to do so.

INTRODUCTION

Seek ye Yahuah while he may be found, call ye upon him while he is near:
Let the wicked forsake his way, and the unrighteous man his thoughts: and
let him return unto Yahuah, and he will have mercy upon him; and to our
Elohim, for he will abundantly pardon. For my thoughts are not your
thoughts, neither are your ways my ways, saith Yahuah. For as the heavens
are higher than the earth, so are my ways higher than your ways, and my
thoughts than your thoughts.

Isaiah 55:6-9

Why just definitions?

If you know anything about me (Huldah), you know that the will of the Father often baffles me. Trying to navigate through what I believe is needed and what the Father has placed on my heart was a hard battle with this particular work. The original intent of this book was to create a series of lessons that each woman could study like a devotional, but once I began, the Father wanted me to do something different. He wanted me to give the tools and for the reader/studier to dig deeper into His word. As much as I enjoy being a companion on your journey of discovery, my partnership will be limited this time. By limited, I mean that I am only transferring the words. It will be your job to study these word meanings in the Word and apply them to your life. My prayer is that through this process you and the Father are able to come closer. I also know that those of you who take this task seriously will grow and abound in ways that will leave your whole household with this testimony:

Her children arise up, and call her blessed; her husband also, and he praiseth her. Many daughters have done virtuously, but thou excellest them all.

Proverbs 31:28-29

**To assist with this process there is now a study guide and videos available. Go to herroyalroots.com for more information.

Building a House

The book is titled <u>*Wisdom Builds*</u> because the function of a "house" is critical in having a Scripturally sound home, and the way that it is constructed is pivotal to its sustainability. Each house contains similar building blocks. For example, each house needs a door for an entrance, each house needs a window for light to illuminate within, each house needs a foundation that is able to endure troubled times, and each house needs strong walls for protection from the elements and dangers without. These are the sheer basics.

Likewise, some things are not a necessity but add character to the home, such as, where you place your window if you choose a tall door or a red door—it's a matter of choice. The same is similar to the nature of this book and how you choose to tackle the word studies. The Hebrew meaning, and the Scriptural context are given. This information will aid in your ability to interpret without violating the text with how you "feel." In Torah, feelings are not applied to commandments and cannot be used to change or negate any part of the Word as it has been delivered from Yahuah.

Why Should I use <u>Wisdom Builds</u> instead of a lexicon or a Biblical dictionary?

The question is going to come up: Why shouldn't I just use a lexicon or dictionary to look up these words? The simple answer would be: How is that working out for us? But the more serious answer is, we have lots of tools and dictionaries that have served a purpose, but they are lacking when it comes to defining words Hebraically for Hebrews. Because each person is in a different place on their walk and understanding of the Hebrew language, I included the Strong's number next to each definition. The numbers are used because there will be times where words are defined, and a person will want to know why these words do not line up with what my dictionary says.

Through study, you will find that often the word that is used in English to define a word could be utilized for several different Hebrew words. For instance, the word for 'law' in Hebrew is Torah; but there are also other words that mean 'teaching' that are also translated as law, leading the reader to believe that each time it says 'law' we should not do those things (not knowing that all 'law' is 'teaching' and all teachings of Scripture are Torah). In a basic word look-up, it will only render the word that directly defines that word in the verse; and not understand all of the other words in Hebrew that have the same meaning, but different function based on context. (E.g. Study 24: chastising) In this study, you will not only learn that chastising is important, but also how every punishment is carried out the same way.

Reading is Fundamental

In each study, you will find the most common Hebrew word for the English translation. The Hebrew word is written in both modern script and pictorial script. The pictorial Hebrew is a tool to aid you in understanding why a Hebrew would have chosen the definition. Remember that Hebraically things are defined based on the elements that are around them (in an Eastern setting). This is why it is pivotal to refrain from defining words based upon where we are in captivity. Our location in the Diaspora (unless you are in the land, and even then, there are perversions that warrant caution) severely limits our ability to interpret the Word based purely on observation because we are in the land of confusion (Babylon), no matter where you are. In knowing this, it is important that you do not rely solely on the one verse that is given to define the word, but that you use a source to look up similar verses that also help to give you additional verses that mean the same thing and see how they are functioning in their different contextual understandings. A great online tool for this is BibleHub.com or if you like a book, Treasury of Scriptural Knowledge. These sources will provide you with all the verses that use the same Hebrew word (conjugation may be different) and how they are translated into English.

***Disclaimer: If you have not read the book in Scripture that a verse is being quoted from, STOP your study and read the book. Context in Scriptural study is in knowing the WHOLE book. Also, if you have not read TORAH (the first five books), STOP! Before you start this study, you need to know that all words and how they will be defined throughout the rest of Scripture have their root in Torah. This is called The Law of First Mention. All the words in the Bible and their root meanings are found in these first five books. You will see this when I have a word that is completely different used in the same way in another part of scripture. This is because for everyone English word there may be 5 Hebrew words that convey the same meaning, but it is the context that separates these words. Each definition in this book will use the most common definition, then you will receive other applicable words that will assist you in understanding how the word would change but the meaning will still be similar. If you do not know how the word was used, then you cannot begin to understand how to apply it.

Ariel, in The Little Mermaid, is an awesome example of what it looks like to not know the function of an object and to run with it. She was just making up words for objects, never knowing how they functioned and what to do with them. In one scene in particular, she sits down with the prince and combs her hair with a fork. That is what it will look like if you have not read Torah and try to understand how these words function just from one verse. I know that was simply an example of a movie, but I think it just helped what I said come to life for someone.

Why is each verse given in Hebrew and English?

First, so you know that I am not making any of this up; second, for you to see where the words are and begin to see them in the text. You will be surprised how much this will help you in learning the language and building your vocabulary. On an even simpler level, this will help you begin to spot the AlephBet if you are just trying to learn what those letters look like in the verses. Finally, you will begin to see the poetry and repetition of words for emphasis that you do not see in English. I encourage you to highlight and write notes in the margins when this happens.

The Importance of Words

These words will help you to connect them to stories in Scripture that will give you a much greater insight into how Yah wants (and does not want) your house to look. Every word in this book will teach both the negatives and positives attached to their implementation and will show the consequences of dysfunction we experience when we fail to properly apply the words to our lives. So, what is remarkable about words? Scripture teaches that Yah's Word sustains everything in the Universe and it is this Word that drives the actions and becomes the motivating factor for all we do.

> *And He is before all things, and by Him all things consist.*
>
> Colossians 1:17

> *In the beginning was the Word, and the Word was with YAH, and the Word was YAH. He was with YAH in the beginning. Through Him all things were made, and without Him nothing was made that has been made.*
>
> John 1:1-3

> *He sendeth forth His commandment upon earth: His Word runneth very swiftly.*
>
> Psalm 147:15

> *By faith we understand that the universe was formed by YAH's command, so that what is seen was not made out of what was visible.*
>
> Hebrews 11:3

> *By the word of Yahuah were the heavens made; and all the host of them by the breath of his mouth.*
>
> Psalm 33:6

When these words are ill-defined or even slightly changed the action and function of those elements (including humans) carrying out the command of the Words are also changed. Imagine getting a blueprint to build a house but every time you try to follow the instruction you find that the definition of the words is different than what you thought they meant. The frustration and the inability to complete the task are inevitable. The same has happened to everyone who has sought to follow the instructions of the words given in organized religion for relationships, spiritual growth, and childrearing. When you aim to do the will of the Word (blueprint), but the definitions change from translation to translation and from teacher to teacher, the frustration keeps you from effectively completing the task. What I have been led to do in this work is to relieve the frustration. The foundational materials are here before you. The nails are pre-packed, the wood is pre-cut, the foundation laid, and the necessary materials delivered to your fingertips. Your job is to follow the directions of the Ruach for how these elements should look in your life and where they need reinforcement.

As you go through each lesson, you will notice that there are New Testament verses that are used either at the beginning or end of the lessons. These verses are there to show you two things; the first is that all words in Scripture must be viewed through a Hebrew lens, and the second is to show you that all words in the Greek can be traced back to an original Hebrew root that will help you better understand how to carry out the ordinances that are restated in the New Testament. By making these terms more concrete, you can transform your mind into the mind of Christ (a Hebraic mind), allowing yourself to think closer to the will of the Father and keep you from praying and operating amiss, which is easily done when the Word of Yah is viewed and carried out through a Western lens.

What is the "Western Lens"?

The Western lens is a viewpoint that operates in form (what something looks like) versus function (what something acts like). The Hebrew language and people are action based. Everything boils down to what something does and not what it looked like when it was doing it. Obedience to the Father and his Word should be the same way. As Hebraic women living in a Western-driven world, we have to stop viewing our function through the lens of the lands of our dispersion and start viewing our actions through the lens of our timeless and unchanging Father. Hebraic women in the Western world are caught on what it looks like to be a Hebrew and not so much on what the function of being a Hebrew is. Our lack of national transformation is based on the fact that we want it to look "right" and we have not yet fully come to grasp with what is right outside of how it is interpreted to us from men who are just as Western as we are. My hope is that as you begin to study these words they will give you the direction toward Hebraic functionality. If it functions, it is Hebrew. If it is dysfunctional, we must reevaluate.

Lastly, this is not a tool that you will go through once and have it. Every word and definition will not make sense on the surface. There are words and definitions here that continue to renew themselves every time I approach them. They gain new meanings, and they transform and stretch me more and more. I am praying that the same happens to you. The reality of the Word is that it does not work for you unless you work for it. Meaning, if you are not working to do what the Word says, then the Word will be stagnant; but as you begin to be obedient to the Word, you will begin to create the blessing and transformation that all of us are seeking in our homes.

Below you will find a key for the format of the definitions and transliterations.

Transliterated Root ↓

Pictographic Script →

מעה (M-AhH) Strong's #4577, 4578/ AHLB #1292 The numbers are where they can be located in each soul

A hidden thing that only Yah knows

An unknown that is known by a higher consciousness ← AHLB (Ancient Hebrew Lexicon of the Strongs (Strongs Concordance)

Gut or lower region

Seat of Consciousness

Internal organs of the lower torso

*And, behold, the word of Yahuah came unto him, saying, this shall not be thine heir; but he that shall come forth out of thine own **bowels** shall be thine heir.*

וְהִנֵּה דְבַר־יְהוָה אֵלָיו לֵאמֹר לֹא יִירָשְׁךָ זֶה כִּי־אִם אֲשֶׁר יֵצֵא **מִמֵּעֶיךָ** הוּא יִירָשֶׁךָ

Genesis 15:4

~**Read Before You Begin**~

I have completed the first two studies for you. These lessons serve as an example of what you can accomplish with each set of words and how you will be able to uncover deeper meaning within familiar texts and verses. Please remember that your journey to building your house will be different but the blueprint and the definition of the words do not change. We cannot add to or take away from the Word (Deut. 4:2), so when in doubt about the application of a word set be sure to err on the side of needing to dive deeper. Be sure to use the Hebrew chart as a guide during your study. Also, never settle for something that cannot be supported by Torah and that you have taken out of context. I pray that in this journey you can use the Word of Yah to unlock His will and function for your house. Don't forget to be patient and to use understanding as you approach each set of words and allow the Ruach to move.

Shalom,

Huldah S. David

Hebrew Definition	Modern Script	Early Script	Picotoral Meaning	Sound	Numerical Value
STRONG, POWER, LEADER, SOURCE,	א	Aleph	OX HEAD	SILENT LETTER	1
HOUSE, IN, FAMILY, WOMB	ב	Bet/Vet	NOMADIC TENT FLOORPLAN	B as in Boy / V as in Vine	2
GO, TRAVEL, WALK, GATHER, CAMEL, CARRY, PERSUE	ג	Gimmel	FOOT	G as in Girl	3
ENTRANCE, DOOR, PATHWAY, DEMENSION, HANG	ד	Dalet	TENT DOOR	D as in Door	4
WINDOW, THE, LOOK, REVEAL, BREATH, SIGH	ה	Hey	MAN WITH RAISED HANDS	H as in Hat	5
ADD, SECURE, HOOK, NAIL, CONNECTION, AND	ו	Vav/Waw/Uau	TENT PEG	V as in Vine / Ow as in WOW	6
PLOW, WEAPON, SWORD, DIG, CUT, THE WORD	ז	Zayin	PLOUGH	Z as in Zebra	7
GROUP, FENCE, OUTSIDE, DIVIDE, SEPARATION, TENT WALL	ח	Chet	TENT WALL	(Soft) CH as in baCH	8
SURROUND, CONTAIN, MUD, SERPENT	ט	Tet	BASKET	T as in Toy	9
ARM, HAND, REACH, WORK, THROW, WORSHIP, DEED	י	Yod	HAND AND ARM	Y as in Yard	10
BEND, OPEN, ALLOW, TAME, CUP, BLESSING, PALM, RECEIVE	כ	Kaph	OPEN PALM	K as in Kite / CH as in BaCH	20
TEACH, INSTRUCT, YOKE, BIND, MOVE, TOWARD, FORCE	ל	Lamed	SHEPHERD STAFF/ GOAD	L as in Light	30
MOTION, CHAOS, MIGHTY, BLOOD	מ	Mem	WATER	M as in Moon	40
CONTINUE, HEIR, SON, MANIFEST, SPERM	נ	Nun	SPROUTING SEED	N as in Night	50
HOLD, PROTECT, PROP, SUPPORT	ס	Samech	THORN	S as in Sun	60
SEE, VISION, PROTECTION, FORCUS, WATCH, EXPERIENCE	ע	Ayin	EYE	SILENT LETTER	70
TALK, BLOW, SCATTER, SPEAK	פ	Peh/Feh	MOUTH	P as in Put / F as in Far	80
WAIT, CHASE, SNARE, HUNT, FISH,	צ	Tsade	MAN ON HIS SIDE	Ts as in nuTs	90
CONDENSE, CIRCLE, TIME	ק	Qoph	SUN AT THE HORIZON	Q as in Queen	100
FIRST, BEGINNING, TOP, HEAD, HIGH, CHEIF	ר	Resh	HEAD OF A MAN	R as in Rake	200
SHARP, PRESS, EAT, CONSUME, DESTROY, FIRE, TWO DANGLERS (BREAST)	ש	Shin/Sin	TWO FRONT TEETH	Sh as in Shore / S as in Sand	300
MARK, SIGN, SIGNATURE, CROSS	ת	Tav/Taw/Tau	TWO CROSSED STICKS	T as in Tall	400

STUDY ONE

Peace: Shalom (שלום)

For I know the thoughts that I think toward you, saith
Yahuah, thoughts of peace, and not of evil, to give you an expected end.
Jeremiah 29:11

P eople often define peace through a very narrow and
often personally bias lens. To many peace is connected
to internal wishes for a moment of isolation to gather
thoughts and/or to rest from the hustle and bustle of daily life.
These individual thoughts and experiences often drive how we
define and react to *peace*, which in turn motivates how we
pursue it. Peace is more than what can be seen on the surface.
Peace is likened to the image of a swan resting peacefully on a
calm glassy lake. The image is often admired and coveted for
its serene effects, but what goes unnoticed is the most
impactful. Though the swan seems to be inactive she is doing
something beneath the water that allows us to experience her
tranquility, she is paddling her feet and moving in a manner
that ensures her position of stillness on the water. Her peace
requires action. Often, when a translator attempts to bring

thought and function to any language something can be lost or poorly conveyed due to the culture and the understating in which it was initially written. And often it is not adequately translated over. Simply put, it can be difficult. Like the swan there is the initial understanding of what peace is from the vantage point of the onlooker but there is a completely different idea of peace when viewed from the position of the swan. If we fail to do this then we can miss what the Highest is trying to show us when it comes to achieving and working toward peace. Fortunately, in this case of translation the English does not leave us far off base from the concrete understanding of the Hebrew. In English, 'peace' is freedom from disturbance, tranquility, cessation of war, or to remain silent. This is a decent definition of peace; however, it is only a partial report. 'Peace' in its current English form does not give any idea of how (like the swan's feet) to achieve peace other than stopping or ceasing an activity or function (similar to merely viewing the outcome of the swan on the water). Yes, there is an intellectual understanding of peace, but as we explore further we should be able to see how to restore, live, and understand peace in every situation.

In Hebrew, the word for 'peace' is seen in two different root words. These two words offer different perspectives to the word 'peace' although they both connect to the same goal. The first is the root *Shlm* and the second is the word *Damah/Damm*. The root for *Shalom* is spelled שלם, and its pictorial spelling is ᴍᴜʃʟʟ. The other word is *Damah* (and *Damm*), spelled (דמה דמם,), and the pictorial spelling is ᴍᴍᴍᴛ (Please refer to the Hebrew chart in the appendix for the pictorial meanings).

Damm is the Hebrew word for blood. The literal translation means to refrain from speech, action, quieting, and repression. The reason these words are used to define blood in an action form is because when a person or animal sheds blood, he/she/it is then silenced. The three-letter root *dalet / mem / hey* means 'to move in a balanced way.' This word symbolizes the same connotation and relation to blood. Blood moves in a balanced way in the Universe. When blood is shed or when life is silenced, it is then given back to the ground; and there must either be restitution paid for the life or it is a cycle which is then complete and causes the body to naturally return to the ground producing peace, rest, and balance. This is the circle of life.

The second root word is the most familiar form of peace. This Hebrew word for peace is *Shalom*. The root of the word is *shin / lamed / final mem*. שלם is defined as being complete or whole. In the Hebraic sense, achieving a positive outcome does not only happen by experiencing positivity. שלם can exist by adding or subtracting possessions, people, health, or comforts for the sake of restitution or recompense. שלם can also mean 'to draw out.' When Yah decides to draw out, it is always to restore something back to its proper position or place. The Father often draws out or quiets one's surroundings to minister to the heart of an individual for an intended purpose. Yah separates those who are dear to Him to repair or restore the inner self. The restoration of the inner self *is* the restoration back to Torah. This is seen respectively in the lives of the children of Israel in their removal from the land which he had given them; land to restore peace between them, the land, and their El. Yah allowed captivity to draw out Israel's sins through chastisement and affliction. This teaches them that there is no better place than within His care. He removed them from the land because they have polluted it with the magnitude of their sins and transgression, so the land cries out to also be restored. Lastly, the Covenant must be renewed and restored. This process is the cyclical process of restitution. It starts and ends with Yahuah. Inner self, place, position, as well as Covenant, are all renewed in the process of shalom. Yahuah desires for each person to achieve *Shalom* in their homes and their inner selves so that they can operate as a vessel of righteousness for His glory. Just as a parent uses different tactics to draw out the best in their children, Yahuah uses the process of silence, removal, and then restoration to bring *Shalom* to His Chosen people.

Application

In the opening Scripture, the Highest is speaking to the prophet Jeremiah regarding His Chosen people who are about to enter into Babylonian captivity. He is giving instructions on what to do while they are in captivity and how to ensure a return from captivity. One may ask, "Why not just keep them out of captivity all together and avoid the grueling monologue?" but that is not how the Father operates. A good father understands that the pursuit of restoration, where peace and tranquility exist, is not always done by keeping silent, avoiding war, or allowing freedom, but sometimes peace comes in obscure, hard-to-grasp-to-the-Western-mind ways. Although the children of Israel are being carried captive into a nation, Yah is commanding that they seek peace where they go and "pray unto Yahuah for peace and in that peace will they have peace" (Jeremiah 29:7). Yahuah goes on to warn them that others will try and convince them of strange doctrines and teachings through prophecy and divination, so they should ignore them, because they are not sent from Him and are liars. Yahuah gives reassurance by stating that after 70 years is accomplished, He will visit the children of Israel and perform His good word toward them and cause them to return to this place (Jeremiah 29:8-10). This verse confirms the process and the cyclical nature of Scripture: peace with the Creator, harmony with one another, and restoration to the promised land as the ultimate goal. Now how we as finite creatures would go about that process and how the infinite Creator brings peace about is a what we must learn and truly embrace.

Yah's view of peace and man's view of peace is completely different. To better understand peace and Yahuah's right-ruling in all circumstances, a person must first remove the mind of a tyrant god and replace it with the image of a loving parent (Father). Knowing that a person first loves you completely changes the way we receive their chastening.

> He who withholds his rod hates his child, but he who loves
> him gives him discipline.
> **Proverbs 13:24**

You will study the Hebrew word chastisement in a later study, but in this current context, it is much better to be disciplined in love than in hate. Many people have a problem with Yahuah and His "blind eye" towards His children during the dangerous and harmful situations over the course of their Diaspora. The sentiment is typically vocalized as "Where was God during slavery?" or "Where was God when these curses were overtaking us?" It is hard to fathom that the Father saw the atrocities which befell on His people as they endured these curses and did nothing. Could a good father sit in his high and lofty seat and watch as children are killed, women are raped, and men are beaten beyond recognition in the name of "God?" How can *that* be love, and how can prosperity flourish in such dysfunction?

Before one jumps to conclusions, a simple refocusing of vantage point clears the blurred egocentric lens that questions the Father's love and motive for chastisement. Captivity serves as the Israelites (and our) chance to view their transgressions as the Father has seen them. It is difficult to see one's wickedness, but watching it play out before you is 20/20. The same way Yahuah watched as the Israelites caused their children to pass through the fire, committed spiritual adultery, whored their children, and all the other transgressions that placed them in this position is how they are now forced to watch it play out before their own eyes. Yahuah is not *witnessing* the mistreatment in a literal sense, because he has already seen it. Instead, He is allowing His children to see what He has seen and is making them live out what they have asked for. The same thing that seemed like pleasure at one's own hands is a nightmare in the hands of the oppressor. In captivity, Yahuah purges through close interaction with sin to give His children a front row seat to their sin so that they will not do it again. The grace and mercy of the Father is that He designates the end of chastisement and gives restoration and peace as the reward for rebalancing and enduring His drawing out process. But just as Yah turned His back as the Messiah hung for restitution (to reconcile or bring *Shalom*), He has also set an appointed end for captivity; but He must turn to allow the completion of His restoration at every level. Due to the curses that the children of Israel heaped upon themselves in the promised land they had to be removed, taken into captivity, cleansed, and then the land and the people can be joined in shalom unto the Father!

> *For I know the thoughts that I think toward you, saith Yahuah, thoughts of peace, and not of evil, to give you an expected end. Then shall ye call upon me, and ye shall go and pray unto me, and I will hearken unto you. And ye shall seek me, and find me when ye shall search for me with all your heart. And I will be found of you, saith Yahuah: and I will turn away your captivity, and I will gather you from all the nations, and from all the places whither I have driven you, saith Yahuah; and I will bring you again into the place whence I caused you to be carried away captive.*
> **Jeremiah 29:11-14**

STUDY TWO

Matrix: Rechem (רחם)

That thou shalt set apart unto Yahuah all that openeth the matrix, and every
firstling that cometh of a beast which thou hast; the males shall be Yahuah's.
Exodus 13:12

In the blockbuster movie, the Matrix, there is a scene where the main character Neo is confronted with the reality of the matrix. From within the matrix, he is made aware that his reality is a simulated experience controlled by a greater force. He must decide to come out. But by merely desiring to get out he faces issues. It was not until his desire met adversity that the subconscious part of him was birthed and he was made alive. In scripture, the birthing process is referred to as passing through the matrix. It is this process of passing through that makes us alive, but it is not what makes man live. Understanding the connection between the process of birthing and the process of awakening is critical. Three major Hebrew words are used to show the stages of the womb and the birth of the subconscious to a physical form. By studying and meditating on these words and definitions, you will have the opportunity to experience the beauty of your body as a vehicle of divine manifestation as well as the portal through which the intentions of another are made manifest. Each word gives the stage of the womb and shows the importance of the "portal" called the woman.

מעה (M-AhH) Strong's #4577, 4578/ AHLB #1292

A hidden thing that only Yah knows

An unknown that is known by a higher consciousness

Gut or lower region

Seat of Consciousness

Internal organs of the lower torso

*And, behold, the word of Yahuah came unto him, saying, this shall not be thine heir; but he that shall come forth out of thine own **bowels** shall be thine heir.*

וְהִנֵּה דְבַר־יְהוָה אֵלָיוֹ לֵאמֹר לֹא
יִירָשְׁךָ זֶה כִּי־אִם אֲשֶׁר יֵצֵא
מִמֵּעֶיךָ הוּא יִירָשֶׁךָ

Genesis 15:4

בטן (BThN) Strong's #990/ AHLB #2015

Pistachio

Protruding stomach

Rounded projection

House which surrounds the seed
Growing belly due to seed inside

*And Jacob's anger was kindled against Rachel: and he said, Am I in Elohim's stead, who hath withheld from thee the fruit of the **womb**?*

וַיִּחַר־אַף יַעֲקֹב בְּרָחֵל וַיֹּאמֶר הֲתַחַת אֱלֹהִים אָנֹכִי אֲשֶׁר־מָנַע מִמֵּךְ פְּרִי־בָטֶן

Genesis 30:2

רחם (R-Hhm) Strong's #7358/ AHLB #2762

The head separated by water
Compassion
Maiden
First born

*That thou shalt set apart unto Yahuah all that openeth the **matrix**, and every firstling that cometh of a beast which thou hast; the males shall be Yahuah's.*

וְהַעֲבַרְתָּ כָל־פֶּטֶר־רֶחֶם
לַיהוָה וְכָל־פֶּטֶר ׀ שֶׁגֶר בְּהֵמָה
אֲשֶׁר יִהְיֶה לְךָ הַזְּכָרִים לַיהוָה:

Exodus 13:12

Application

The womb, seed, and Yah are all a part of a triune covenant. Yah guides the subconscious and the desire. The man gives the physical seed, and the woman takes the subconscious will of the father and the desire of the male and manifests a child that will be nurtured and given back to the one who knew he or she before they were even knit in the womb. Three forms of the womb with one (Echad) purpose.

> *As for me, behold, my covenant is with thee, and thou shalt be a father of many nations. Neither shall thy name any more be called Abram, but thy name shall be Abraham; for a father of many nations have I made thee. And I will make thee exceeding fruitful, and I will make nations of thee, and kings shall come out of thee. And I will establish my covenant between me and thee and thy seed after thee in their generations for an everlasting covenant, to be an Elohim unto thee, and to thy seed after thee. And Yah said unto Abraham, As for Sarai thy wife, thou shalt not call*

WISDOM BUILDS • 15

*her name Sarai, but Sarah shall her name be. And
I will bless her, and give thee a son also of her:
yea, I will bless her, and she shall be a mother of
nations; kings of people shall be of her.*

Gen 17:4-7;15-16

Submit: Anah (ענה)

Submitting yourselves one to another in the fear of YAH.
Ephesians 5:21

ענה (AhNH) Strong's #6031,6033 / AHLB #1359

Watch intently

Concentrate

Humble

Be occupied or busied with

To be in a position that makes one look up

*And the angel of Yahuah said unto her, Return to thy mistress, and **submit** thyself under her hands.*

ג וַיֹּאמֶר לָהֹ מַלְאַךְ יְהֹוָה שׁוּבִי
אֶל־גְּבִרְתֵּךְ **וְהִתְעַנִּי** תַּחַת יָדֶיהָ

Genesis 16:9

<u>**כחש** (KHhSh) Strong's #3584, 3585,3586/ AHLB #2257</u>

Pretend obedience

To correct

Deny justified demands

To withhold something to get a desired outcome

Withholding to cause leanness

To withhold what you have in your hand to afflict another

Then Sarah ***<u>denied</u>****, saying, I laughed not; for she was afraid. And he said, Nay; but thou didst laugh.*

וַתְּכַחֵשׁ שָׂרָה ׀ לֵאמֹר לֹא צָחַקְתִּי
כִּי ׀ יָרֵאָה וַיֹּאמֶר ׀ לֹא כִּי צָחָקְתְּ

Genesis 18:15

<u>**רפס** (RPS) Strong's #7511,7512,7515/ AHLB #2786</u>

Stomping down

The head trampling or stomping with speech

Impoverish or lower

Cause to cover

control

Rebuke the company of spearmen, the multitude of the bulls, with the calves of the people, *till every one* **submit** himself with pieces of silver: scatter thou the people *that* delight in war.

גְּעַר חַיַּת קָנֶה עֲדַת אַבִּירִים ׀
בְּעֶגְלֵי עַמִּים **מִתְרַפֵּס** בְּרַצֵּי־
כָסֶף בִּזַּר עַמִּים קְרָבוֹת יֶחְפָּצוּ

Psalm 68:30

Build: Banah (בנה)

That thou shalt set apart unto Yahuah all that openeth the matrix, and every firstling that cometh of a beast which thou hast; the males shall be Yahuah's.
Exodus 13:12

בנה (B-NH) Strong's #1124, 1129/ AHLB #1037

Forming

Having children

Producer

Endowing

Structure built for occupation

Repairer

Builder

*Then the rib which Yahuah Elohim had taken from man He **made** into a woman, and He brought her to the man.*

וַיִּ֫בֶן יְהוָ֣ה אֱלֹהִ֣ים ׀ אֶת־הַצֵּלָ֛ע
אֲשֶׁר־לָקַ֥ח מִן־הָֽאָדָ֖ם לְאִשָּׁ֑ה
וַיְבִאֶ֖הָ אֶל־הָֽאָדָֽם

Genesis 2:22

<u>בון</u> (BWN) Strong's #8394/ AHLB #1037

Intelligence
The skill of mind and hands
Planning and building of a house
Mediate
Consider
Teacher

*So that you incline your ear to wisdom, and apply your heart to **understanding**;*

לְהַקְשִׁ֣יב לַחָכְמָ֣ה אָזְנֶ֑ךָ תַּטֶּ֥ה
לִ֝בְּךָ֗ <u>לַתְּבוּנָֽה</u>

Proverbs 2:2

<u>בנן</u> (BNN) Strong's #1146,1147/ AHLB #1037
Building or housing a family
The structure that houses the family
The continuing of the house requires a womb and a
seed

*Now there was a wall around the outside of the
temple. In the man's hand was a measuring rod
six cubits long, each being a cubit and a
handbreadth; and he measure the width of the
wall **structure**, one rod; and height, one rod.*

וְהִנֵּה חוֹמָה מִחוּץ לַבַּיִת סָבִיב ׀
סָבִיב וּבְיַד הָאִישׁ קְנֵה הַמִּדָּה שֵׁשׁ־
אַמּוֹת בָּאַמָּה וָטֹפַח וַיָּמָד אֶת־רֹחַב
הַבִּנְיָן קָנֶה אֶחָד וְקוֹמָה קָנֶה אֶחָד:

Ezekiel 40:5

<u>בין</u> (BYN) Strong's #995,996,997,998,999,1143/ AHLB #1037
Understand
Discernment between two things or sides

Having insight
Revealing or making known
Understanding interactions of elements

*Now therefore, let Pharaoh select a **discerning** and wise man, and set him over the land of Egypt.*

וְעַתָּה֙ יֵרֶ֣א פַרְעֹ֔ה אִ֖ישׁ **נָב֣וֹן** וְחָכָ֑ם וִישִׁיתֵ֖הוּ עַל־אֶ֥רֶץ מִצְרָֽיִם

Genesis 41:33

פנה (PN-Kh) Strong's #6847,6437,3942,6440/ AHLB #1382

Safe guarding
Join elements

And Pharaoh called Joseph's name Zaphnath-**Paaneah**.

וַיִּקְרָ֨א פַרְעֹ֤ה שֵׁם־יוֹסֵף֙ צָֽפְנַ֣ת **פַּעְנֵ֔חַ** וַיִּתֶּן־ל֣וֹ אֶת־אָֽסְנַ֗ת בַּת־פּ֥וֹטִי פֶ֛רַע כֹּהֵ֥ן אֹ֖ן לְאִשָּׁ֑ה וַיֵּצֵ֥א יוֹסֵ֖ף עַל־אֶ֥רֶץ מִצְרָֽיִם

Genesis 41:45

Family: Shapach (שפח)

But if any provide not for his own, and specially for those of his own house,
he hath denied the faith, and is worse than an infidel.
1 Timothy 5:8

שפח (ShPHh) Strong's #8198,4940/ AHLB #2863

Family

Join to a maiden

Increase by attaching

A female who gives her body to serve in building a

clan

But you shall go to my father's house and to my
family, *and take a wife for my son.*

אִם־לֹא אֶל־בֵּית־אָבִי תֵּלֵךְ וְאֶל־
מִשְׁפַּחְתִּי וְלָקַחְתָּ אִשָּׁה לִבְנִי
Genesis 24:38

†ᘔᗗ⊕

בית (BYT) Strong's #1004,1005/ AHLB #1045
House
Place of protection
Family mark
Tribe
People
 Nest
Jail
Grave

*Then Yahuah said to Noah, "Come into the ark, you and all your **household**, because I have seen that you are righteous before Me in this generation.*

וַיֹּאמֶר יְהֹוָה֙ לְנֹ֔חַ בֹּֽא־אַתָּ֥ה וְכׇל־
בֵּיתְךָ֖ אֶל־הַתֵּבָ֑ה כִּֽי־אֹתְךָ֥ רָאִ֛יתִי
צַדִּ֥יק לְפָנַ֖י בַּדּ֥וֹר הַזֶּֽה
Genesis 7:1

טפף (ThPP) Strong's #2952,2945/ AHLB #1201
Unsteady steps

The skipping or stumbling of children

*Moreover your **little ones**, which ye said should be a prey, and your children, which in that day had no knowledge between good and evil, they shall go in thither, and unto them will I give it, and they shall possess it.*

וְטַפְּכֶם֩ אֲשֶׁ֨ר אֲמַרְתֶּ֜ם לָבַ֣ז יִהְיֶ֗ה וּבְנֵיכֶ֡ם אֲשֶׁ֣ר לֹא־יָדְעוּ֩ הַיּוֹם֙ ט֣וֹב וָרָ֔ע הֵ֚מָּה יָבֹ֣אוּ שָׁ֔מָּה וְלָהֶ֣ם אֶתְּנֶ֔נָּה וְהֵ֖ם יִירָשֽׁוּהָ

Deuteronomy 1:39

<u>אלף</u> (ALP) Strong's #441 / AHLB #2001

Guide
Yoke
Receive from others
Lack independence
Leader whose followers are dependent

*But it was thou, a man mine equal, my **guide**, and mine acquaintance.*

וְאַתָּ֣ה אֱנ֣וֹשׁ כְּעֶרְכִּ֑י **אַלּוּפִ֗י** וּמְיֻדָּעִֽי

Psalm 55:13

STUDY SIX

Woman: Isha (אשה)

אשה (AShH) Strong's #801,802/ AHLB #1021

Foundation
Black
Strong pressing down
Fire shaped material
Supporting pillar
Created material

*And if the **woman** is not willing to follow you, then you will be released from tis oath; do not take my son back there.*

וְאִם־לֹא תאבֶה **הָאשה** לָלֶכֶת
אַחֲרֶיךָ וְנִקִּיתָ מִשְּׁבֻעָתִי זְאת רַק
אֶת־בְּנִי לֹא תָשֵׁב שמה

Genesis 24:8

𐤉𐤔𐤔𐤕

נשה (NSh) Strong's #5382/ AHLB #1320

Continually pressing
A debt or deception which causes oppression
Obligate
Give up rights
Submitting
More delicate sex
Cause to forget

Joseph called the name of the first-born Manasseh: "For Yah has made me __forget__ all my toil and all my father's house."

וַיִּקְרָא יוֹסֵף אֶת־שֵׁם הַבְּכוֹר
מְנַשֶּׁה כִּי־נַשַּׁנִי אֱלֹהִים אֶת־כָּל־
עֲמָלִי וְאֵת כָּל־בֵּית אָבִי

Genesis 41:51

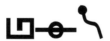

נקב (NQB) Strong's #5344,5345,5347 / AHLB #1416,2430

hole
Designated one
Appoint

To make whole in order to deposit
To place a ring or hole in

Then Jehoiada the priest took a chest, bored a **hole** *in its lid, and set it beside the altar, on the right side as one comes into the house of Yahuah; and the priests who kept the door put there all the money brought into the house of Yahuah.*

וַיִּקַּ֞ח יְהוֹיָדָ֤ע הַכֹּהֵן֙ אֲר֣וֹן אֶחָ֔ד
וַיִּקֹּ֥ב חֹ֖ר בְּדַלְתּ֑וֹ וַיִּתֵּ֤ן אֹתוֹ֙ אֵ֣צֶל
הַמִּזְבֵּ֔חַ [בַּיָּמִ֖ין כ] (מִיָּמִ֖ין ק)
בְּבוֹא־אִישׁ֙ בֵּ֣ית יְהֹוָ֔ה וְנָֽתְנוּ־שָׁ֤מָּה
הַכֹּֽהֲנִים֙ שֹׁמְרֵ֣י הַסַּ֔ף אֶת־כָּל־
הַכֶּ֖סֶף הַמּוּבָ֥א בֵית־יְהֹוָֽה

2 Kings 12:9

STUDY SEVEN

Man: Zakar (זכר)

זכר (NSh) Strong's #234, 1798-9,2142-3,2145-6/ AHLB #1320

Remember

Historian

Mindful

Mention through speech

Speak on the behalf of another

Speak for the family

*Three times in the year all thy **males** shall appear before Yahuah ELOHIM.*

שָׁלֹשׁ פְּעָמִים בַּשָּׁנָה יֵרָאֶה כָּל־
זְכוּרְךָ אֶל־פְּנֵי הָאָדֹן ׀ יְהוָה

Exodus 23:17

<u>בֵּן</u> (BN) Strong's #1121,1123,1247/ AHLB #1037

Continuing of the house

Lasting

Seed of the house

And Abraham circumcised his **son** Isaac being eight days **old**, as Elohim had commanded him.

וַיָּ֣מָל אַבְרָהָם֮ אֶת־יִצְחָק֒ **בְּנ֔וֹ בֶּן־** שְׁמֹנַ֣ת יָמִ֔ים כַּאֲשֶׁ֛ר צִוָּ֥ה אֹת֖וֹ אֱלֹהִֽים

Genesis 21:4

<u>אדם</u> (A-DM) Strong's #119,120/ AHLB #1082

Ground

Earthy

Likeness

Flowing of Blood

Rich in Minerals

Mankind

And Elohim said, Let us make **man** *in our image, after our likeness: and let them have dominion over the fish of the sea, and over the fowl of the*

air, and over the cattle, and over all the earth, and over every creeping thing that creepeth upon the earth.

וַיֹּאמֶר אֱלֹהִים נַעֲשֶׂה **אָדָם**
בְּצַלְמֵנוּ כִּדְמוּתֵנוּ וְיִרְדּוּ בִדְגַת הַיָּם
וּבְעוֹף הַשָּׁמַיִם וּבַבְּהֵמָה וּבְכָל־הָאָרֶץ
וּבְכָל־הָרֶמֶשׂ הָרֹמֵשׂ עַל־הָאָרֶץ

Genesis 1:26

אִישׁ <u>(AYSh)</u> Strong's #376,380/ AHLB #1021

Charred after being burned in fire

fire

black

black of night

pillar

man with proven character

*And Adam knew Eve his wife; and she conceived, and bare Cain, and said, I have gotten a **man** from Yahuah.*

וְהָאָדָם יָדַע אֶת־חַוָּה אִשְׁתּוֹ וַתַּהַר וַתֵּלֶד
אֶת־קַיִן וַתֹּאמֶר קָנִיתִי **אִישׁ** אֶת־יְהוָה

Genesis 4:1

<u>גבר</u> (GBR) Strong's #1396/ AHLB #2052

Authority

Prevail

Warrior

Control through physical strength

Overpower

Victorious

Master

Strong

And Cush begat Nimrod: he began to be a **<u>mighty</u>** one in the earth.

וְכוּשׁ יָלַד אֶת־נִמְרֹד הוּא הֵחֵל
לִהְיוֹת **<u>גִּבֹּר</u>** בָּאָרֶץ

Genesis 10:8

STUDY EIGHT

King: Malak (מלך)

𒀭 / 𐤋 𐤌

מלך (MLK) Strong's #4427-8, 4430-1/ AHLB #2340

Walk among the people
Reign
Counsel/Advising
Consider differing views
Judge
Intellectual head of the people

And Elohim said unto Abraham, As for Sarai thy wife,
thou shalt not call her name Sarai, but
Sarah *shall her name be.*

וַיֵּצֵא **מֶלֶךְ**־סְדֹם֙ לִקְרָאתוֹ֙ אַחֲרֵי
שׁוּב֗וֹ מֵהַכּוֹת֙ אֶת־כְּדָר־לָעֹ֔מֶר וְאֶת־
הַמְּלָכִ֖ים אֲשֶׁ֣ר אִתּ֑וֹ אֶל־עֵ֣מֶק שָׁוֵ֔ה
ה֖וּא עֵ֥מֶק הַמֶּֽלֶךְ׃

Genesis 14:17

Queen: Sarah (שרה/סרה)

שרה/סרה (S-RH) Strong's #8283/ AHLB #1342

Nobel woman
Turning heads (people)
Exerting Superior Power
Supporting the head
Turn the leaders to Yah
Revolt

*And Elohim said unto Abraham, As for Sarai thy wife, thou shalt not call her name Sarai, but **Sarah** shall her name be.*

וַיֹּ֤אמֶר אֱלֹהִים֙ אֶל־אַבְרָהָ֔ם שָׂרַ֣י
אִשְׁתְּךָ֔ לֹא־תִקְרָ֥א אֶת־שְׁמָ֖הּ שָׂרָ֑י
כִּ֥י **שָׂרָ֖ה** שְׁמָֽהּ

Genesis 17:15

‡山ﬡ Ⱶﬡ

<u>מלכת</u> (ML-KH) Strong's #4433,4436/ AHLB #2340

Advising

Counsel

Consult

Of the people

Walking among the people

And the thing was known to Mordecai, who told it unto Esther the **queen***; and Esther certified the king thereof in Mordecai's name.*

וַיִּוָּדַ֤ע הַדָּבָר֙ לְמָרְדֳּכַ֔י וַיַּגֵּ֖ד לְאֶסְתֵּ֣ר **הַמַּלְכָּ֑ה** וַתֹּ֧אמֶר אֶסְתֵּ֛ר לַמֶּ֖לֶךְ בְּשֵׁ֥ם מָרְדֳּכָֽי

Esther 2:22

STUDY TEN

Virtuous: Chayil (חיל)

Who can find a virtuous woman? for her price is far above rubies.
Proverbs 31:10

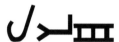

חיל (HhYL) Strong's #2426,2427,2428,2429,2430/ AHLB #1173
Power
A hole through which the enemy enters a city
Strength and wealth of a person
bulwark

*Mark ye well her **bulwarks**, consider her palaces; that ye may tell it to the generation following.*

ו שִׁיתוּ לִבְּכֶם | **לְחֵילָה** פַּסְּגוּ אַרְמְנוֹתֶיהָ לְמַעַן תְּסַפְּרוּ לְדוֹר אַחֲרוֹן
Psalm 48:13

Father: AB (אב)

Submitting yourselves one to another in the fear of YAH.
Ephesians 5:21

אב (AB) Strong's #1-4 / AHLB #1002

Strength of the House
To Stand
Fruit
Pole/Pillar
Desire
Wineskin

Therefore shall a man leave his __father__ and his mother, and shall cleave unto his wife: and they shall be one flesh.

עַל־כֵּן֙ יַֽעֲזָב־אִ֔ישׁ אֶת־אָבִ֖יו וְאֶת־
אִמּ֑וֹ וְדָבַ֣ק בְּאִשְׁתּ֔וֹ וְהָי֖וּ לְבָשָׂ֥ר
אֶחָֽד

Genesis 2:2

מֵן (MN) Strong's #539-40, 4478/ AHLB #1290-C

Number

Firm

Sure

Kind

Blood Continues

Portion

Pillar

Support

*Who can **count** the dust of Jacob, and the number of the fourth part of Israel? Let me die the death of the righteous, and let my last end be like his!*

מִי **מָנָה֙** עֲפַר יַעֲקֹ֔ב וּמִסְפָּר אֶת־
רֹ֖בַע יִשְׂרָאֵ֑ל תָּמֹ֤ת נַפְשִׁי֙ מ֣וֹת
יְשָׁרִ֔ים וּתְהִ֥י אַחֲרִיתִ֖י כָּמֹֽהוּ

Numbers 23:10

STUDY TWELVE

Mother: Em (אם)

אם(מ)ם <u>(AM) Strong's #517,519,520,521/ AHLB #1013</u>

Be dependent

Point of Departure

Arm

Bind

Glue

The arms that hold things together

Strong water

Giving physical and spiritual life

And Adam called his wife's name Eve; because
she was the __mother__ of all living.

וַיִּקְרָא הָאָדָם שֵׁם אִשְׁתּוֹ חַוָּה כִּי
הִוא הָיְתָה **אֵם** כָּל־חָי

Genesis 3:20

אמה (A-MH) Strong's #517,519,520,521/ AHLB #1013

Serve
Pillar
Bondwoman
Support

Wherefore she said unto Abraham, Cast out this
bondwoman *and her son: for the son of this*
bondwoman shall not be heir with my
son, even with Isaac.

וַתֹּאמֶר֙ לְאַבְרָהָ֔ם גָּרֵ֛שׁ **הָאָמָ֥ה**
הַזֹּ֖את וְאֶת־בְּנָ֑הּ כִּ֣י לֹ֤א יִירַשׁ֙ בֶּן־
הָאָמָ֣ה הַזֹּ֔את עִם־בְּנִ֖י עִם־יִצְחָֽק

Genesis 21:10

STUDY THIRTEEN

Help: Azar (עזר)

Whoso findeth a wife findeth a good thing, and obtaineth favour of the Yah.
Proverbs 18:22

עזר (AhZR) Strong's #5826,5828,5833/ AHLB #2535

Restrain

Support

Ally

Progress

Help to reduce responsibilities

Gird

*And Yahuah Elohim said, It is not good that the man should be alone; I will make him an **help meet** for him.*

וַיֹּ֨אמֶר יְהוָ֣ה אֱלֹהִים֒ לֹא־ט֛וֹב הֱיֹ֥ות הָֽאָדָ֖ם לְבַדֹּ֑ו אֶֽעֱשֶׂהּ־לֹּ֥ו **עֵזֶר** כְּנֶגְדֹּֽו

Genesis 2:18

STUDY FOURTEEN

Rib: Tsela (צלע)

צלע (Ts-LAh) Strong's #5967,6760,6761,6763/ AHLB #2664

Surrounding wall

Side

Limp

Fall

Favoring one side

Beam

*And the **rib**, which Yahuah Elohim had taken from man, made he a woman, and brought her unto the man.*

וַיִּ֩בֶן֩ יְהוָ֨ה אֱלֹהִ֧ים ׀ אֶת־**הַצֵּלָ֛ע**
אֲשֶׁר־לָקַ֥ח מִן־הָֽאָדָ֖ם לְאִשָּׁ֑ה
וַיְבִאֶ֖הָ אֶל־הָֽאָדָֽם
Genesis 2:22

\

Deceived: Nasha (נשה)

And Adam was not deceived, but the woman being deceived was in the transgression.
1 Timothy 2:14

<u>נשה</u> (NSh) Strong's #4860,4855,5383,5386/ AHLB #1320

Loan

Debt

Deception

Pressing the seed

Beguile

The enemy shall not __exact__ upon him; nor the son of wickedness afflict him.

לֹא־**יַשָּׁא** אוֹיֵב בּוֹ וּבֶן־עַוְלָה לֹא
יְעַנֶּנּוּ

Psalm 89:22

𐤔𐤟𐤁𐤁𐤟(𐤔)

שגג(ה) (ShG) Strong's #4870,4879,7683-4,7686 / AHLB #1436

Sin

Err

To cause to repeat

Double burden

Error made on accident or unintentionally

Careless mistake

*And if ye have **erred**, and not observed all these commandments, which Yahuah hath spoken unto Moses*

וְכִי **תִשְׁגּוּ** וְלֹא תַעֲשׂוּ אֵת כָּל־
הַמִּצְוֺת הָאֵלֶּה אֲשֶׁר־דִּבֶּר יְהוָה
אֶל־מֹשֶׁה

Numbers 15:22

התל (H-TL) Strong's #2048,4123/ AHLB #1495

Debt that causes oppression

To hang

Deflate

Mock

And Delilah said unto Samson, Behold, thou hast **mocked** *me, and told me lies: now tell me, I pray thee, wherewith thou mightest be bound.*

וַתֹּ֨אמֶר דְּלִילָה֙ אֶל־שִׁמְשׁ֔וֹן הִנֵּה֙ **הֵתַ֣לְתָּ** בִּ֔י וַתְּדַבֵּ֥ר אֵלַ֖י כְּזָבִ֑ים עַתָּה֙ הַגִּ֣ידָה־נָּ֣א לִ֔י בַּמֶּ֖ה תֵּאָסֵֽר

Judges 16:10

Meek: Anav (ענו)

&

Quiet: Shataq (שתק)

Whose adorning let it not be that outward adorning of plaiting the hair, and of wearing of gold, or of putting on of apparel; But let it be the hidden man of the heart, in that which is not corruptible, even the ornament of a meek and quiet spirit, which is in the sight of God of great price.

1 Peter 3:3-4

<u>ענו</u> (Ah-NW) Strong's #6035,6037-8/ AHLB #1359

For the sake of

State of poverty

Lowliness

Gentle

Guarding something of importance

Watching and willing to die for the seed

Experienced and secured to the seed

Oppressed
*(Now the man Moses was very **meek**, above all the men which were upon the face of the earth.)*

וְהָאִישׁ מֹשֶׁה [**עָנָו** כ] (**עָנָיו** ק) מְאֹד מִכֹּל הָאָדָם אֲשֶׁר עַל־פְּנֵי הָאֲדָמָה

Number 12:3

‑⊙‑†Ш

שתק (ShTQ) Strong's #8367,120/ AHLB #2889

Silence

Still

Calming

Satisfying rightful need

*Then are they glad because they be **quiet**; so he bringeth them unto their desired haven.*

וַיִּשְׂמְחוּ כִי־**יִשְׁתֹּקוּ** וַיַּנְחֵם אֶל־ מְחוֹז חֶפְצָם

Psalm 107:30

ש⅃⅃Y

שלו (ShLW) Strong's #7951,7959,7961-3,/ AHLB #1021

Prosper

Drawing out what is needed

Assur

Being complete

Undisturbed peace

Placenta

*Peace be within thy walls, and **prosperity** within thy palaces.*

יְהִי־**שָׁלוֹם** בְּחֵילֵךְ לְוָֹה בְּאַרְמְנוֹתָיִךְ

Psalm 122:7

רגע (GBR) Strong's #7280-2,4774/ AHLB #2752

Restrain

Cease movement

Careful movement

Stir up from rest

The moving of water

Wink of an eye

Refreshing

*And among these nations shalt thou find no **ease**, neither shall the sole of thy foot have rest: but Yahuah shall give thee there a trembling heart, and failing of eyes, and sorrow of mind.*

וּבַגּוֹיִם הָהֵם לֹא **תַרְגִּיעַ** וְלֹא־
יִהְיֶה מָנוֹחַ לְכַף־רַגְלֶךָ וְנָתַן יְהוָה לְךָ
שָׁם לֵב רַגָּז וְכִלְיוֹן עֵינַיִם וְדַאֲבוֹן נָפֶשׁ

Deuteronomy 28:65

שָׁאַן (ShAN) Strong's #7599/ AHLB #1474
Separation
Sharpen
Rest
Fortunate
Protected

*Our soul is exceedingly filled with the scorning **of those that are at ease**, and with the contempt of the proud.*

רַבַּת שָׂבְעָה־לָהּ נַפְשֵׁנוּ הַלַּעַג
הַשַּׁאֲנַנִּים הַבּוּז לִגְאֵיוֹנִים

Psalm 123:4

Keeper: Shamar (שמר)

Here is the patience of the saints: here are they that keep the
commandments of Yahuah, and the faith of Yahusha.
Revelation 14:12

<u>שמר</u> (ShMR) Strong's #8104-5,8108/ AHLB #2853

Protect

Keep from danger

Guard

Save life

Preserve

Watchman

Being aware

Building a protected wall around

Only take heed to thyself, and **keep** *thy soul
diligently, lest thou forget the things which thine
eyes have seen, and lest they depart from thy
heart all the days of thy life: but teach them thy
sons, and thy sons' sons;*

רַ֗ק הִשָּׁ֣מֶר לְךָ֩ וּשְׁמֹ֨ר נַפְשְׁךָ֜
מְאֹ֗ד פֶּן־תִּשְׁכַּ֨ח אֶת־הַדְּבָרִ֜ים
אֲשֶׁר־רָא֣וּ עֵינֶ֗יךָ וּפֶן־יָס֨וּרוּ֙
מִלְּבָ֣בְךָ֔ כֹּ֖ל יְמֵ֣י חַיֶּ֑יךָ וְהוֹדַעְתָּ֥ם
לְבָנֶ֖יךָ וְלִבְנֵ֥י בָנֶֽיךָ

Deuteronomy 4:9

<u>נטר</u> (NThR) Strong's #5201,5202/ AHLB #2400

Protecting

Maintain

Grudge

*He will not always chide: neither will he **keep** his anger for ever.*

לֹא־לָנֶ֥צַח יָרִ֑יב וְלֹ֖א לְעוֹלָ֣ם <u>**יִטּֽוֹר**</u>

Psalm 103:9

<u>נצר</u> (NTsR) Strong's #5341,5341/ AHLB #2429

A pressing in or on something

To close in with pressure

Watching

Controlling

Protected bud- guarding the seed as it grows

Branch

Movement

Hidden thing

*And there shall come forth a rod out of the stem of Jesse, and a **Branch** shall grow out of his roots:*

יֵצֵא חֹטֶר מִגֵּזַע יִשָׁי <u>וְנֵצֶר</u>
מִשָּׁרָשָׁיו יִפְרֶה

Isaiah 11:1

STUDY EIGHTEEN

Crown: Ketar (עטר)

שׂ†𐤀

כתר (KTR) Strong's #3803-5/ AHLB #2300

To surround

Encircle

Crown

Top of a pillar as a crown

Place a sign or covenant on the head

Royal covenant

And the king loved Esther above all the women, and she obtained grace and favour in his sight more than all the virgins; so that he set the royal **crown** *upon her head, and made her queen instead of Vashti.*

וַיֶּאֱהַב הַמֶּלֶךְ אֶת־אֶסְתֵּר מִכָּל־הַנָּשִׁים
וַתִּשָּׂא־חֵן וָחֶסֶד לְפָנָיו מִכָּל־הַבְּתוּלֹת
וַיָּשֶׂם **כֶּתֶר**־מַלְכוּת בְּרֹאשָׁהּ וַיַּמְלִיכֶהָ
תַּחַת וַשְׁתִּי

Esther 2:17

<u>עטר</u> (AhThR) Strong's #5849,5850/ AHLB #2538

To bestow a crown

Encircle

Wreath

Sign of authority

Who redeemeth thy life from destruction; who **<u>crowneth</u>** *thee with lovingkindness and tender mercies;*

הַגּוֹאֵל מִשַּׁחַת חַיָּיְכִי **<u>הַמְעַטְּרֵכִי</u>** חֶסֶד וְרַחֲמִים

Psalm 103:4

<u>נזר</u> (NZR) Strong's #4502,5144,5145/ AHLB #2390

Separate

Warning/ teaching to be set apart

Nazarite

Uncut hair

Consecrate

Dedicate

Woman's hair/ hair

*And thou shalt put the mitre upon his head, and
put the holy **crown** upon the mitre.*

וְשַׂמְתָּ הַמִּצְנֶפֶת עַל־רֹאשׁוֹ לֹ
וְנָתַתָּ אֶת־**נֵזֶר** הַקֹּדֶשׁ עַל־הַמִּצְנָפֶת

Exodus 29:6

STUDY NINETEEN

Roots: Shoresh (שרש)

שרש (ShRSh) Strong's #8327/ AHLB #2883

Connect elements

Take root

To plant and allow to flourish

*Thou preparedst room before it, and didst cause it to **take deep root**, and it filled the land.*

פִּנִּיתָ לְפָנֶיהָ **וַתַּשְׁרֵשׁ** שָׁרָשֶׁיהָ וַתְּמַלֵּא־אָרֶץ Psalm 80:9

נתק (NTQ) Strong's #5423-4,5428/ AHLB #2455

Tear apart

Transplant

Destroy roots
Removal of the seed (covenant)
Pull to a breaking point

Let us break their bands asunder, *and cast*
away their cords from us.

נְנַתְּקָה אֶת־מוֹסְרוֹתֵימוֹ וְנַשְׁלִיכָה
מִמֶּנּוּ עֲבֹתֵימוֹ

Psalm 2:3

נתש (NTSh) Strong's #5428/ AHLB #1321,2456
Uprooting
Pluck
Remove

*And Yahuah **rooted them out** of their land in*
anger, and in wrath, and in great indignation,
and cast them into another land, as it is this day.

וַיִּתְּשֵׁם יְהוָה מֵעַל אַדְמָתָם
בְּאַף וּבְחֵמָה וּבְקֶצֶף גָּדוֹל
וַיַּשְׁלִכֵם אֶל־אֶרֶץ אַחֶרֶת כַּיּוֹם
הַזֶּה

Deuteronomy 29:28

עקר (GhQR) Strong's #6133,6135/ AHLB #2905

Barren

Make lame

Impotent

Pull root out of the ground

*He maketh the **barren** woman to keep*
house, and to be a joyful mother of children.
Praise ye Yahuah.

מֽוֹשִׁיבִ֨י ׀ **עֲקֶ֬רֶת** הַבַּ֗יִת אֵֽם־
הַבָּנִ֥ים שְׂמֵחָ֗ה הַֽלְלוּ־יָֽהּ

Psalm 113:9

STUDY TWENTY

Ground: Adamah (אדמה)

__אדם__ (ADM) Strong's #126,127,1819,1823-4/ AHLB #1082

Rich in minerals
Yielding sustenance
Tilled
Earth substance for building or constructing
Likeness
Using nutrients from one place to create another

How shall I give thee up, Ephraim? how shall I deliver thee, Israel? how shall I make thee as __Admah__? how shall I set thee as Zeboim? mine heart is turned within me, my repentings are kindled together.

אֵיךְ אֶתֶּנְךָ אֶפְרַיִם אֲמַגֶּנְךָ֙
יִשְׂרָאֵל אֵיךְ אֶתֶּנְךָ __כְאַדְמָה__

אֲשִׂימְךָ כִּצְבֹאיִם נֶהְפַּךְ עָלַי לִבִּי
יַחַד נִכְמְרוּ נִחוּמָי

Hosea 11:8

עפר (AhPR) Strong's #6083/ AHLB #2565

Being earthy
Powder
Earth colored

*And Yahuah Elohim formed man of the **dust** of the ground, and breathed into his nostrils the breath of life; and man became a living soul.*

וַיִּיצֶר יְהוָֹה אֱלֹהִים אֶת־
הָאָדָם **עפר** מִן־הָאֲדָמָה וַיִּפַּח
בְּאַפָּיו נִשְׁמַת חַיִּים וַיְהִי הָאָדָם
לְנֶפֶשׁ חַיָּה

Genesis 2:7

ש/סהד (SHD) Strong's #7717/ AHLB #1326

Testify/ Testimony

A portion of ground for planting or setting up tents
A place for building structure
Field
Foundation
Level place
Record that lays a foundation about an event

Also now, behold, my witness is in heaven, **and my record** *is on high.*

גַּם־עַתָּה הִנֵּה־בַשָּׁמַיִם עֵדִי וְ**שָׂהֲדִי** בַּמְּרוֹמִים

Job 16:19

עור (AhWR) Strong's #5783-5,6174/ AHLB #2905
See a man
Covering for the soul
Brilliance
Glow or burn
Awakening
Naked
Skin
Blind

*And they were both **naked**, the man and his wife, and were not ashamed.*

וַיִּהְיוּ שְׁנֵיהֶם֙ **עֲרוּמִּים** הָֽאָדָ֖ם
וְאִשְׁתּ֑וֹ וְלֹ֖א יִתְבֹּשָֽׁשׁוּ

Genesis 2:25

STUDY TWENTY-ONE

Truth: Emet (אמת)

Yahusha saith unto him, I am the way, the truth, and the life: no man cometh unto the Father, but by me.

John 14:6

מנה (M-NH) Strong's #4490/ AHLB #1290

Kind

Portion

Allocation

Belong

Collection

*Yahuah is the **portion** of mine inheritance and of my cup: thou maintainest my lot.*

יְהוָֹה **מְנָת**־חֶלְקִי וְכוֹסִי אַתָּה תּוֹמִיךְ גּוֹרָלִי

Psalm 16:5

<u>אמן</u> (AMN) Strong's #539/ AHLB #1290

Sure

Seed

Depend upon

Rely on

Affirmation

Stand firm

Strength through blood

Faithful

*And the people **believed**: and when they heard that Yahuah had visited the children of Israel, and that he had looked upon their affliction, then they bowed their heads and worshipped.*

וַ<u>יַּאֲמֵן</u> הָעָם וַיִּשְׁמְעוּ כִּי־
פָקַד יְהֹוָה אֶת־בְּנֵי יִשְׂרָאֵל וְכִי
רָאָה אֶת־עָנְיָם וַיִּקְּדוּ וַיִּשְׁתַּחֲווּ

Exodus 4:31

<u>נצב</u> (NTsB) Strong's #5324/ AHLB #2426

Stand/ Wall

Protecting against harsh elements
Stem of a tree
Fixed
Enduring
Erect

*And, behold, Yahuah **stood** above it, and said,
I am Yahuah Elohim of Abraham thy father, and
the Elohim of Isaac: the land whereon thou liest,
to thee will I give it, and to thy seed;*

וְהִנֵּ֨ה יְהֹוָ֜ה **נִצָּ֣ב** עָלָיו֮ וַיֹּאמַר֒
אֲנִ֣י יְהֹוָ֗ה אֱלֹהֵי֙ אַבְרָהָ֣ם אָבִ֔יךָ
וֵֽאלֹהֵ֖י יִצְחָ֑ק הָאָ֗רֶץ אֲשֶׁ֤ר אַתָּה֙
שֹׁכֵ֣ב עָלֶ֔יהָ לְךָ֥ אֶתְּנֶ֖נָּה וּלְזַרְעֶֽךָ

Genesis 28:13

אמנה (A-MW-NH) Strong's #530,4327,4480-1/ AHLB #1290
Stability
What is firm
What is true about an individual
Where a person is from

*But Moses' hands were heavy; and they took a
stone, and put it under him, and he sat thereon;*

*and Aaron and Hur stayed up his hands, the one on the one side, and the other on the other side; and his hands were **steady** until the going down of the sun.*

וִידֵ֤י מֹשֶׁה֙ כְּבֵדִ֔ים וַיִּקְחוּ־אֶ֛בֶן וַיָּשִׂ֥ימוּ תַחְתָּ֖יו וַיֵּ֣שֶׁב עָלֶ֑יהָ וְאַהֲרֹ֨ן וְח֜וּר תָּֽמְכ֣וּ בְיָדָ֗יו מִזֶּ֤ה אֶחָד֙ וּמִזֶּ֣ה אֶחָ֔ד וַיְהִ֥י יָדָ֛יו **אֱמוּנָ֖ה** עַד־בֹּ֥א הַשָּֽׁמֶשׁ

Exodus 17:12

קשט (QShTh) Strong's #7189/ AHLB #2739
Weigh
Balance/ Fair
Scale
Outer self
Moral truth
Covenant
Lasting
Caring for

That I might make thee know the **certainty** of the words of truth; that thou mightest answer the words of truth to them that send unto thee?

לְהוֹדִיעֲךָ קֹשְׁטְ אִמְרֵי אֱמֶת
לְהָשִׁיב אֲמָרִים אֱמֶת לְשֹׁלְחֶיךָ

Proverbs 22:21

Pregnant: Harah (הרה)

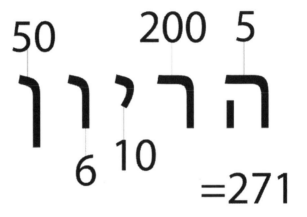

Hebrew word for pregnancy is *herayon* with a gematria of 271 (Strongs #2032)

הר (HR) Strong's #2022/ AHLB #1112

High

Hill

Mountain raising out of the ground

Thou shalt bring them in, and plant them in the **mountain** of thine inheritance, *in* the place, O

Yahuah, *which* thou hast made for thee to dwell in, *in* the Sanctuary, O Yahuah, *which* thy hands have established.

תְּבִאֵמוֹ וְתִטָּעֵמוֹ֙ **בְּהַ֤ר**
נַחֲלָֽתְךָ֙ מָכ֧וֹן לְשִׁבְתְּךָ֛ פָּעַ֖לְתָּ
יְהוָ֑ה מִקְּדָ֕שׁ אֲדֹנָ֖י כּוֹנְנ֥וּ יָדֶֽיךָ

Exodus 15:17

ﺀ

הרה (HRH) Strong's #2029/ AHLB #1112
Source of instruction
Implant and absorb seed
Conceive a child

And Adam knew Eve his wife; and she **conceived**, and bare Cain, and said, I have gotten a man from Yahuah.

וְהָ֣אָדָ֔ם יָדַ֖ע אֶת־חַוָּ֣ה אִשְׁתּ֑וֹ
וַתַּ֙הַר֙ וַתֵּ֣לֶד אֶת־קַ֔יִן וַתֹּ֕אמֶר קָנִ֥יתִי
אִ֖ישׁ אֶת־יְהוָֽה

Genesis 4:1

Trust/Refuge: Batach (בטח)

Trust in Yahuah with all thine heart; and lean not unto thine own understanding.

Proverbs 3:5

חסה (HhSH) Strong's #2347,2620,3187,4268/ AHLB #1176

Trust

Look forward to with confidence

Support shelter

Spare

The history of ones family

And he shall say, Where *are* their
gods, *their* rock in whom they **trusted**,

וְאָמַר אֵי אֱלֹהֵימוֹ צוּר **חָסָיוּ** בוֹ

Deuteronomy 32:37

⊞⊗⊡⊞⊞

בטח (BThHh) Strong's #982,983/ AHLB #2013
Feeling secure
Melon protected by thick rind
Confidence
Cling

He **trusted** in the Yahuah Elohim of Israel; so that after him was none like him among all the kings of Judah, nor *any* that were before him.

וְאַחֲרָ֗יו **בָּטַח** אֱלֹהֵי־יִשְׂרָאֵ֖ל בַּֽיהוָ֑ה
יְהוּדָ֔ה מַלְכֵ֣י בְּכֹל֙ כָּמֹ֔הוּ לֹא־הָיָ֣ה
לְפָנָ֖יו הָי֥וּ וַאֲשֶׁ֖ר
2 Kings 18:5

Discretion: Sekel
(שכל/סכל)

As a jewel of gold in a swine's snout, so is a fair woman which is without discretion.
Proverbs 11:22

ﬡﬡﬡﬡﬡ

ש/סכל (SKL) Strong's #7919-20,7922/ AHLB #2477
Ability to consider
Weigh information for gain
Understanding
Sense
Prudence

And when the woman saw that the tree *was* good for food, and that it *was* pleasant to the eyes, and a tree to be desired **to make one wise**, she took of the fruit thereof, and did eat, and gave also unto her husband with her; and he did eat.

וַתֵּרֶא הָאִשָּׁה כִּי טוֹב הָעֵץ
לְמַאֲכָל וְכִי תַאֲוָה־הוּא לָעֵינַיִם

וְנֶחְמָד הָעֵץ֮ **לְהַשְׂכִּיל**
וַתִּקַּח מִפִּרְיוֹ וַתֹּאכַל וַתִּתֵּן גַּם־
לְאִישָׁהּ עִמָּהּ וַיֹּאכַל

Genesis 3:6

שפט (ShPTh) Strong's #4941,8196,8199,8200/ AHLB #2864

Judge
Created order and harmony
Regulate
Making decisions

The fear of Yahuah *is* clean, enduring for ever:
the **judgments** of
Yahuah *are* true *and* righteous altogether.

יִרְאַת יְהֹוָה ׀ טְהוֹרָה֮ עוֹמֶדֶת
לָעַד **מִשְׁפְּטֵי**־יְהֹוָה אֱמֶת צָדְקוּ
יַחְדָּו

Psalm 19:9

Love: Ahav (אהב)

So ought men to love their wives as their own bodies. He that loveth his wife loveth himself.

Ephesians 5:28

<u>אהב</u> (AHB) Strong's #157,160,1890/ AHLB #1094

Love

Devoted completely to another

Relating intimately

Providing for the house

Conforming or being agreeable

Stimulate desire

Privileged gifts or burden

*And Isaac brought her into his mother Sarah's tent, and took Rebekah, and she became his wife; and he **loved** her: and Isaac was comforted after his mother's death.*

וַיְבִאֶהָ יִצְחָק הָאֹהֱלָה שָׂרָה אִמּוֹ
וַיִּקַּח אֶת־רִבְקָה וַתְּהִי־לוֹ לְאִשָּׁה
וַיֶּאֱהָבֶהָ וַיִּנָּחֵם יִצְחָק אַחֲרֵי אִמּוֹ

Genesis 24:67

ⵙⵍⵄ

עגב (AhGB) Strong's #5689,5691,5748/ AHLB #2523

Flirt

Sensuous tones

Lustfulness

Flute (piped instrument)

*And when thou art spoiled, what wilt thou do?
Though thou clothest thyself with crimson,
though thou deckest thee with ornaments of
gold, though thou rentest thy face with painting,
in vain shalt thou make thyself fair;* **thy lovers** *will
despise thee, they will seek thy life.*

וְאַתִּי כ] (וְאַתְּ ק) שָׁדוּד מַה־
תַּעֲשִׂי כִּי־תִלְבְּשִׁי שָׁנִי כִּי־תַעְדִּי עֲדִי־
זָהָב כִּי־תִקְרְעִי בַפּוּךְ עֵינַיִךְ לַשָּׁוְא
תִּתְיַפִּי מָאֲסוּ־בָךְ **עֹגְבִים** נַפְשֵׁךְ
יְבַקֵּשׁוּ

Jeremiah 4:30

𐤑𐤌𐤐𐤌

הבב (HhB) Strong's #2243,2245/ AHLB #116

Hide
Bosom
Refuge
Wall of the house
Cherish
Passion
Protecting
Satisfaction
Love dutifully

Yea, he **loved** the people; all his saints *are* in thy hand: and they sat down at thy feet; *every one* shall receive of thy words.

אַף **חֹבֵב** עַמִּים כָּל־קְדֹשָׁיו בְּיָדֶךָ
וְהֵם תֻּכּוּ לְרַגְלֶךָ יִשָּׂא מִדַּבְּרֹתֶיךָ

Deuteronomy 33:3

דד (DWD) Strong's #1730-1,1733/ AHLB #1073

Support
Service needs

Friend
Beloved
Joyous love
Breasts
Boiling passion

Let him kiss me with the kisses of his mouth: for thy **love** *is* better than wine.

יִשָּׁקֵ֙נִי֙ מִנְּשִׁיק֣וֹת פִּ֔יהוּ כִּי־
טוֹבִ֥ים **דֹּדֶ֖יךָ** מִיָּֽיִן

Song of Solomon 1:2

חשק (HhShQ) Strong's #2836-8/ AHLB #2219
Desire to hold close
Hugging
Encircling
Affection
Connection
Attached

Yahuah did not set his **love** upon you, nor choose you, because ye were more in number than any people; for ye *were* the fewest of all people:

לֹא מֵרֻבְּכֶם מִכָּל־הָעַמִּים **חָשַׁק**
יְהוָה בָּכֶם וַיִּבְחַר בָּכֶם כִּי־אַתֶּם הַמְעַט
מִכָּל־
הָעַמִּים

Deuteronomy 7:7

רחם (RHhM) Strong's #7356-60/ AHLB #2762
Protect from harm
Empathizing
Mercy
Tender love
Pity

And Elohim Almighty give you **mercy** before
the man, that he may send away your other
brother, and Benjamin. If I be bereaved *of my
children*, I am bereaved.

וְאֵל שַׁדַּי יִתֵּן לָכֶם **רַחֲמִים**
לִפְנֵי הָאִישׁ וְשִׁלַּח לָכֶם אֶת־
אֲחִיכֶם אַחֵר וְאֶת־בִּנְיָמִין וַאֲנִי
כַּאֲשֶׁר שָׁכֹלְתִּי שָׁכָלְתִּי

Genesis 43:14

רעה (RAhH) Strong's #7453, 7462-4,7470/ AHLB #1453

Tend

Satisfy

Spiritual sustenance

Unified

Shepherd

Growing

Knowing thoughts

Concerned

Man watches

Thou knowest my downsitting and mine uprising, thou **understandest** my thought afar off.

אַתָּה יָדַעְתָּ שִׁבְתִּי וְקוּמִי בַּנְתָּה **לְרֵעִי** מֵרָחוֹק

Psalm 139:2

Chastise: Yasar (יסר)

He that spareth his rod hateth his son: but he that loveth him chasteneth him betimes.

Proverbs 13:24

יסר (Y-SR) Strong's #631,3256,4148/ AHLB #1342

To correct

To make a change in direction through correction

Turning head of a child or student

Punish

Instruct

Set limits/restrain

*And if ye will not be **reformed** by me by these things, but will walk contrary unto me; Then will I also walk contrary unto you, and will punish you yet seven times for your sins.*

וְאִם־בְּאֵלֶּה לֹא **תִוָּסְרוּ** לִי
וַהֲלַכְתֶּם עִמִּי קֶרִי וְהָלַכְתִּי אַף־

אֲנִי עִמָּכֶם בְּקֶרִי וְהִכֵּיתִי אֶתְכֶם
גַּם־אָנִי שֶׁבַע עַל־חַטֹּאתֵיכֶם

Leviticus 26:23-24

𐤋𐤔𐤔𐤌𐤌

יכח (YKHh) Strong's #3198 AHLB #1238

Chastise

Correct with a firm hand

Reprove

Rebuke

Plead/reason

Admonish

*For whom Yahuah loveth he **correcteth**; even as a father the son in whom he delighteth.*

כִּי אֶת אֲשֶׁר יֶאֱהַב יְהוָה **יוֹכִיחַ**
וּכְאָב אֶת־בֵּן יִרְצֶה

Proverbs 3:12

𐤓𐤔𐤔𐤊

כשר (KShR) Strong's #3787-8/ AHLB #2294

Prepare

Connect Properly

Being Skillful
Bonding
Act Right
In Line
Prosperity
Success

*Elohim setteth the solitary in families: he
bringeth out those which are **bound** with
chains: but the rebellious dwell in a dry land.*

אֱלֹהִים ׀ מֹושִׁיב יְחִידִים ׀
בַּיְתָה מֹוצִיא אֲסִירִים **בַּכֹּושָׁרֹות**
אַךְ סֹורֲרִים שָׁכְנוּ צְחִיחָה

Psalm 68:6

𐤔𐤄𐤄𐤄𐤄

כחח (KHHk) Strong's #3581,8433/ AHLB #1238
Exert power
Be strong
Right hand

*And in very deed for this cause have I raised thee
up, for to shew in thee my **power**; and that my
name may be declared throughout all the earth.*

וְאוּלָם בַּעֲבוּר זֹאת הֶעֱמַדְתִּיךָ
בַּעֲבוּר הַרְאֹתְךָ אֶת־**כֹּחִי** וּלְמַעַן סַפֵּר
שְׁמִי בְּכָל־
הָאָרֶץ.

Exodus 9:16

יגע (Y-GAh) Strong's #3021-3/ AHLB #1062

Tire

Worn out

Weary

Exert one's self

labor

*And I will come upon him while he is **weary** and weak handed, and will make him afraid: and all the people that are with him shall flee; and I will smite the king only:*

וְאָבוֹא עָלָיו וְהוּא **יָגֵעַ** וּרְפֵה
יָדַיִם וְהַחֲרַדְתִּי אֹתוֹ וְנָס כָּל־הָעָם
אֲשֶׁר־אִתּוֹ וְהִכֵּיתִי אֶת־הַמֶּלֶךְ
לְבַדּוֹ

2 Samuel 17:2

יגה (YGH) Strong's #3013-4/ AHLB #1210
Suffer
Sorrow
Removing

The ways of Zion do mourn, because none come to the solemn feasts: all her gates are desolate: her priests sigh, her virgins are **afflicted**, *and she is in bitterness.*

דַּרְכֵי צִיֹּון אֲבֵלֹות מִבְּלִי בָּאֵי מֹועֵד
כָּל־שְׁעָרֶיהָ שֹׁומֵמִין כֹּהֲנֶיהָ נֶאֱנָחִים
בְּתוּלֹתֶיהָ **נּוּגֹות** וְהִיא מַר־לָהּ

Lamentations 1:4

ישר (YShR) Strong's #3474/ AHLB #1480
Straighten
Faithful to duty
Tightly secure
Navel cord
Loosen cord

*Therefore, I **esteem***

all thy precepts concerning all things to

be right; and I hate every false way.

עַל־כֵּן ׀ כָּל־פִּקּוּדֵי כֹל **יִשָּׁרְתִּי**

כָּל־אֹרַח שֶׁקֶר שָׂנֵאתִי

Psalm 119:128

Wisdom: Chakam (חכם)

𐤌𐤀𐤔𐤌𐤌

<u>חכם</u> (HhKM) Strong's #2449-52,2454 AHLB #2159

Accumulate knowledge

Absorb knowledge

Be wise

Learn

*The fear of Yahuah is the beginning of **wisdom**: and the knowledge of the holy is understanding.*

תְּחִלַּת **חָכְמָה** יִרְאַת יְהוָה וְדַעַת קְדֹשִׁים בִּינָה

Proverbs 9:10

<u>בין</u> (BYN) Strong's #995-9,1143/ AHLB #1037

Exert power

Be strong
Right hand

Also Jonathan David's uncle was a counseller, a **wise** *man, and a scribe: and Jehiel the son of Hachmoni was with the king's sons:*

וִיהוֹנָתָן דּוֹד־דָּוִיד יוֹעֵץ אִישׁ־**מֵבִין** וְסוֹפֵר הוּא וִיחִיאֵל בֶּן־חַכְמוֹנִי עִם ־בְּנֵי הַמֶּלֶךְ

1 Chronicles 27:32

טַעַם (Th-AhM) Strong's #2938,2940/ AHLB #2236
Reason
Perceive
Sensing
Tasting
Distinguishing thoughts
Advice

And blessed be thy **advice**, *and blessed be thou, which hast kept me this day from coming to shed blood, and from avenging myself with mine own hand.*

וּבָרוּךְ **טַעְמֵךְ** וּבְרוּכָה אָתְּ
אֲשֶׁר כְּלִתִנִי הַיּוֹם הַזֶּה מִבּוֹא
בְדָמִים וְהשֵׁעַ יָדִי לִי

1 Samuel 25:33

⫸/⊔⊔⊔⊔/⫷

סכל/שכל (SKL) Strong's #7919/ AHLB #2477

Consider
Wisdom
Understand
Prosper
Success

*I will behave myself **wisely** in a perfect way. O
when will you come unto me? I will walk within
my house with a perfect heart.*

אַשְׂכִּילָה ׀ בְּדֶרֶךְ תָּמִים מָתַי
תָּבוֹא אֵלָי אֶתְהַלֵּךְ בְּתָם־לְבָבִי
בְּקֶרֶב בֵּיתִי

Psalm 101:2

Order: Arak (ערך)

ערך (AhRK) Strong's #4634,6186-7/ AHLB #2576
Arrange side by side
Being an equal
Plan
Preparation
Furnish

*But she had brought them up to the roof of the house, and hid them with the stalks of flax, which she had **laid in order** upon the roof*

וְהִיא הֶעֱלָתַם הַגָּגָה וַתִּטְמְנֵם בְּפִשְׁתֵּי הָעֵץ **הָעֲרֻכוֹת** לָהּ עַל־הַגָּג

Joshua 2:6

כִּין (KWN) Strong's #3559,3561 AHLB #1244
Firm
Foundation
Guide
Fixed by words

Order *my steps in thy word: and let not any iniquity have dominion over me.*

פְּעָמַי **הָכֵן** בְּאִמְרָתֶךָ וְאַל־
תַּשְׁלֶט־בִּי כָל־אָוֶן
Psalm 119:133

דָּבַר (D-BR) Strong's #1696/ AHLB #2093
The order in which something is performed
Arrangement
Bees (observationally)
Regulation
Collecting
Gathering
Subdue
Speak a command

*Then Judah came near unto him, and said, Oh my lord, let thy servant, I pray thee, speak a **word** in my lord's ears, and let not thine anger burn against thy servant: for thou art even as Pharaoh.*

וַיִּגַּשׁ אֵלָיו יְהוּדָה וַיֹּאמֶר בִּי
אֲדֹנִי יְדַבֶּר־נָא עַבְדְּךָ **דבר** בְּאָזְנֵי
אֲדֹנִי
וְאַל־יִחַר אַפְּךָ בְּעַבְדֶּךָ כִּי
כָמוֹךָ כְּפַרְעֹה

Genesis 44:18

𐤑𐤅𐤀𐤔

<u>צוה</u> (TsWH) Strong's #4687,6680/ AHLB #1397
Command
Appoint
Charge
Delegate authority

*Because that Abraham obeyed my voice, and kept my charge, my **commandments**, my statutes, and my laws.*

עֵקֶב אֲשֶׁר־שָׁמַע אַבְרָהָם בְּקֹלִי
וַיִּשְׁמֹר מִשְׁמַרְתִּי **מִצְוֹתַי** חֻקּוֹתַי
הָאָרֶץ.וְתוֹרֹתָי

Genesis 26:5

סדר (SDR) Strong's #5468, 7713/ AHLB #2468

Arrange

Set in order

Establish law

A row of planks when constructing a house

An army

*A land of darkness, as darkness itself; and of the shadow of death, without any **order**, and where the light is as darkness.*

אֶרֶץ עֵיפָתָה | כְּמוֹ אֹפֶל
צַלְמָוֶת וְלֹא **סְדָרִים** וַתֹּפַע כְּמוֹ־
אֹפֶל

Job 10:22

‎ෆ/ᰌ/ᰌ

‎שלב (ShLB) Strong's #7947-8/ AHLB 2840

Step

Level

Bound

Joined

Equal order

*Two tenons shall there be in one board, **set in order** one against another: thus shalt thou make for all the boards of the tabernacle.*

‎שְׁתֵּי יָדֹות לַקֶּרֶשׁ הָאֶחָד
‎**מְשֻׁלָּבֹת** אִשָּׁה אֶל־אֲחֹתָהּ כֵּן
‎תַּעֲשֶׂה לְכֹל קַרְשֵׁי הַמִּשְׁכָּן

Exodus 26:17

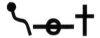

‎תקן (TQN) Strong's #3474/ AHLB #1480

Ready

Complete

Straightening

Participating

Be made straight

Put in place
Proper alignment

*That which is crooked cannot **be made straight**:*
and that which is wanting cannot be numbered…

וְחֶסְרוֹן **לְתַקֵּן** לֹא־יוּכַל מְעֻוָּת
לְהִמָּנוֹת לֹא־יוּכַל
Ecclesiastes 1:15

STUDY TWENTY-NINE

Teach: Yarah (ירה)

𐤉𐤀𐤔𐤄

ירה <u>(Y-RH) Strong's #3138,3384/ AHLB #1227</u>

Cast

Shoot forth to a particular place

Early rain

Throwing of a hand to a direction to live or walk

Awe or fear of calamity

Point in the way of life

*That I will give you the rain of your land in his due season, **the first rain** and the latter rain, that thou mayest gather in thy corn, and thy wine, and thine oil.*

וְנָתַתִּ֧י מְטַֽר־אַרְצְכֶ֛ם בְּעִתּ֖וֹ
יוֹרֶ֣ה וּמַלְק֑וֹשׁ וְאָסַפְתָּ֣ דְגָנֶ֔ךָ
וְתִירֹשְׁךָ֖ וְיִצְהָרֶֽךָ

Deuteronomy 11:14

בִין (BNN) Strong's #995 AHLB #1244
Consider carefully
Diligently consider
Discern
Penetrate to the core
Thorough reasoning
Making known

*My son, attend unto my wisdom, and bow thine ear to **my understanding**:*

בְּנִי לְחָכְמָתִי הַקְשִׁיבָה **לִתְבוּנָתִי** הַט־אָזְנֶךָ

Proverbs 5:1

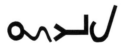

לִיץ (LYTS) Strong's #3887/ AHLB #1271
Interpret
Ambassador
Mediator
The authority of the tongue
Speaking a language and needing an interpreter

And they knew not that Joseph understood them; for he spake unto them by __an interpreter.__

וְהֵם֙ לֹ֣א יָ֣דְע֔וּ כִּ֥י שֹׁמֵ֖עַ יוֹסֵ֑ף כִּ֥י **הַמֵּלִ֖יץ** בֵּינֹתָֽם

Genesis 42:23

עדי

יָדַע (YDA) Strong's #3045/ AHLB #1085

To have an intimate relationship with a person, idea, or experience
Be aware
Knowledge
Recognizing
Door of the eye

For Elohim doth know that in the day ye eat thereof, then your eyes shall be opened, and ye shall be as gods, __knowing__ good and evil.

כִּ֚י יֹדֵ֣עַ אֱלֹהִ֔ים כִּ֗י בְּיוֹם֙ אֲכָלְכֶ֣ם מִמֶּ֔נּוּ וְנִפְקְח֖וּ עֵינֵיכֶ֑ם וִהְיִיתֶם֙ כֵּֽאלֹהִ֔ים **יֹדְעֵ֖י** ט֥וֹב וָרָֽע

Genesis 3:5

אלף (ALPh) Strong's #502/ AHLB #2001
Guide, yoke, learn
To learn by example
To bring forth 100 fold
Younger taught by the more experienced
Husband
Friend

*If not, hearken unto me: hold thy peace, and I shall **teach** thee wisdom.*

אִם־אַיִן אַתָּה שְׁמַע־לִי הַחֲרֵשׁ
וַאֲאַלֶּפְךָ חָכְמָה

Job 33:33

זהר (ZHR) Strong's #2094-5/ AHLB #1158
Warn of limits
Admonish
Shine light in a direction or onto something
Heed

Moreover by them is thy servant **warned**: *and in keeping of them there is great reward.*

גַּם־עַבְדְּךָ **נִזְהָר** בָּהֶם בְּשָׁמְרָם עֵקֶב רָב

Psalm 19:11

<u>שנן</u> (ShNN) Strong's #8150/ AHLB #1474

Sharpen

Focus

Teaching repeatedly

Tearing apart and digesting

Precision

Direct speech

<u>And thou shalt teach them</u> *diligently unto thy children, and shalt talk of them when thou sittest in thine house, and when thou walkest by the way, and when thou liest down, and when thou risest up.*

וְשִׁנַּנְתָּם לְבָנֶיךָ וְדִבַּרְתָּ בָּם בְּשִׁבְתְּךָ בְּבֵיתֶךָ וּבְלֶכְתְּךָ בַדֶּרֶךְ וּבְשָׁכְבְּךָ וּבְקוּמֶךָ

Deuteronomy 6:7

למד

לְמַד (LMD) Strong's #3925,3928,4451/ AHLB 2311

Learn

Learn by chastisement or goading

Instruct

Expert

Skillful

Directing oxen in yoke

Learn from behavior

Habituating

Disciple/ Student

*Now therefore hearken, O Israel, unto the statutes and unto the judgments, which I **teach** you, for to do them, that ye may live, and go in and possess the land which Yahuah Elohim of your fathers giveth you.*

וְעַתָּה יִשְׂרָאֵל שְׁמַע אֶל־הַחֻקִּים וְאֶל־
הַמִּשְׁפָּטִים אֲשֶׁר אָנֹכִי **מְלַמֵּד** אֶתְכֶם
לַעֲשׂוֹת לְמַעַן תִּחְיוּ וּבָאתֶם וִירִשְׁתֶּם
אֶת־הָאָרֶץ אֲשֶׁר יְהוָה אֱלֹהֵי אֲבֹתֵיכֶם
נֹתֵן לָכֶם:

Deuteronomy 4:1

שׁ

שׂכל (SKL) Strong's #7919,7920,7922/ AHLB #2477

Understand

Adapt to needs

Causing to succeed

Absorb information

Instructing for comprehension

Knowingly guiding

Acting rationally

*O that they were wise, that they **understood** this, that they would consider their latter end!*

אִלוּ חָכְמוּ יַשְׂכִּילוּ זֹאת יָבִינוּ
לְאַחֲרִיתָם

Deuteronomy 32:29

STUDY THIRTY

"Weaker" Vessel: Keli (כלי)

Likewise, ye husbands, dwell with them according to knowledge, giving honour unto the wife, as unto the weaker vessel, and as being heirs together of the grace of life; that your prayers be not hindered.
1 Peter 3:7

עש/ו

כלה (K-LH) Strong's #3618 / AHLB #1242

Strive to attain

Yearn

Organ of Yearning

Bride

Consummation

Complete/whole

Tame for the yoke

*Thou has ravished my heart, my sister, my **spouse**; thou hast ravished my heart with one of thine eyes, with one chain of thy neck.*

לִבַּבְתִּנִי אֲחֹתִי **כַלָּה**
לִבַּבְתִּינִי [בְּאַחַד כ] (בְּאַחַת ק)
מֵעֵינַיִךְ בְּאַחַד
עֲנָק מִצַּוְּרֹנָיִךְ

Song of Solomon 4:9

<u>תאנה</u> (TA-NH) Strong's #579,8385 AHLB #1014

Produce

Sending for one to have an encounter

Opportunity

Donkey (wild ass)

*A wild ass used to the wilderness, that snuffeth
up the wind at her pleasure; in her occasion
who can turn her away? all they that seek her
will not weary themselves; in her month they
shall find her.*

פֶּרֶה ׀ לִמֻּד מִדְבָּר בְּאַוַּת [נַפְשׁוֹ כ]
(נַפְשָׁהּ ק) שָׁאֲפָה רוּחַ **תַּאֲנָתָהּ** מִי
יְשִׁיבֶנָּה כָּל־מְבַקְשֶׁיהָ לֹא יִיעָפוּ
בְּחָדְשָׁהּ יִמְצָאוּנְהָ

Jeremiah 2:24

<u>נבל</u> (NBL) Strong's #5035/ AHLB #1035,2639

Interpret

Ambassador

Mediator

The authority of the tongue

Speaking a language and needing an interpreter

*And he shall break it as the breaking of the potters' **vessel** that is broken in pieces; he shall not spare: so that there shall not be found in the bursting of it a sherd to take fire from the hearth, or to take water withal out of the pit.*

וּשְׁבָרָהּ כְּשֵׁבֶר **נֵבֶל** יוֹצְרִים כָּתוּת לֹא יַחְמֹל וְלֹא־יִמָּצֵא בִמְכִתָּתוֹ חֶרֶשׂ לַחְתּוֹת אֵשׁ מִיָּקוּד וְלַחְשֹׂף מַיִם מִגֶּבֶא

Isaiah 30:14

Beautiful: Yapheh (יפה)

Thou art all fair, my love; there is no spot in thee.
Song of Solomon 4:7

<u>יפה</u> (YPH) Strong's #3302-3/ AHLB #1224

Goes beyond the normal
A wonder
Excite the senses

And it came to pass, when he was come near to enter into Egypt, that he said unto Sarai his wife, Behold now, I know that thou art a **fair** *woman to look upon:*

וַיְהִ֕י כַּאֲשֶׁ֥ר הִקְרִ֖יב לָב֣וֹא
מִצְרָ֑יְמָה וַיֹּ֙אמֶר֙ אֶל־שָׂרַ֣י אִשְׁתּ֔וֹ
הִנֵּה־נָ֣א יָדַ֔עְתִּי כִּ֛י אִשָּׁ֥ה **יְפַת־**
מַרְאֶ֖ה אָֽתְּ

Genesis 12:11

טוֹב (THWB) Strong's #2876,2895,2898 AHLB #1186

Advance benefit to man

Good and pleasant

Functional

Happy

Healthy

Treat well

Surround the house

Being purposeful

Being beautiful

*And he said, I will make all my **goodness** pass before thee, and I will proclaim the name of Yahuah before thee; and will be gracious to whom I will be gracious, and will shew mercy on whom I will shew mercy.*

וַיֹּאמֶר אֲנִי אַעֲבִיר כָּל־**טוּבִי** עַל־
פָּנֶיךָ וְקָרָאתִי בְשֵׁם יְהוָה לְפָנֶיךָ
וְחַנֹּתִי אֶת־ אֲשֶׁר אָחֹן וְרִחַמְתִּי
אֶת־אֲשֶׁר אֲרַחֵם

Exodus 33:19

<u>**יפע**</u> (YPAh) Strong's #3313/ AHLB #1384

Radiate

Emerge from darkness

Brightness awaken

Send out beams

*Out of Zion, the perfection of **beauty**, Elohim hath shined.*

מִצִּיּוֹן מִכְלַל־<u>**יֹפִי**</u> אֱלֹהִים הוֹפִיעַ

Psalm 50:2

<u>**נאה**</u> (N-AH) Strong's #4998,5000/ AHLB #130

Pleasant

Comely

Appropriate

Lovely

Pleasant habitation

Comfort

*Rejoice in Yahuah, O ye righteous: for praise is **comely** for the upright..*

רַנְּנוּ צַדִּיקִים בַּיהוָה לַיְשָׁרִים
נָאוָה תְהִלָּה

Psalm 33:1

<u>פרה</u> (P-RH) Strong's #6500,6509/ AHLB #1388

Fruitful

Increase

Reveal the seed

Decoration

Progeny

*Thy wife shall be as a **fruitful** vine by the sides of thine house: thy children like olive plants round about thy table.*

.

אֶשְׁתְּךָ ׀ כְּגֶפֶן **פֹּרִיָּה**בְּיַרְכְּתֵי
בֵיתֶךָ בָּנֶיךָ כִּשְׁתִלֵי זֵיתִים סָבִיב
לְשֻׁלְחָנֶךָ

Psalm 128:3

<u>עטר</u> (AhThR) Strong's #5849,5850/ AHLB #2538

Wreath

Sign of Authority
Wrapped
Encircle (Guarded)
Bounds of Territory
Distinguish

*She shall give to thine head an ornament of grace: a **crown** of glory shall she deliver to thee.*

תִּתֵּן לְרֹאשְׁךָ לִוְיַת־חֵן
עֲטֶרֶת תִּפְאֶרֶת תְּמַגְּנֶךָּ

Proverbs 4:9

<u>פאר</u> (P-AR) Strong's #6289/ AHLB #1388

Distinguish
Standout
Distinctive
See in good light
Bravery
Blackness
Turban upon the head
Honor

*In that day the Lord will take away the **bravery** of their tinkling   ornaments about   their   feet,* *and their cauls, and their round tires like the moon,*

בַּיּוֹם הַהוּא יָסִיר אֲדֹנָי אֵת **תִּפְאֶרֶת**
הָעֲכָסִים וְהַשְּׁבִיסִים וְהַשַּׁהֲרֹנִים

Isaiah 3:18

Vanity: Ayn (אין)

Beware lest any man spoil you through philosophy and vain deceit, after the tradition of men, after the rudiments of the world, and not after Christ.
Colossians 2:8

אין (AYN) Strong's #369 AHLB #1014

Vanity

Absent of

Using the power of the lower region

Creative work for empty purposes

Mischief

Unable to do or have something

Work with no results

*But Sarai was barren; she had **no** child.*

וַתְּהִי שָׂרַי עֲקָרָה **אֵין** לָהּ וָלָד

Genesis 11:30

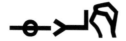

ריק (RYQ) Strong's #7385-6/ AHLB #1456

Empty of all contents

Take away from nutrients

I also will do this unto you; I will even appoint over you terror, consumption, and the burning ague, that shall consume the eyes, and cause sorrow of heart: and ye shall sow your seed __in vain__, for your enemies shall eat it.

אַף־אֲנִי אֶעֱשֶׂה־זֹּאת לָכֶם
וְהִפְקַדְתִּי עֲלֵיכֶם בֶּהָלָה אֶת־
הַשַּׁחֶפֶת וְאֶת־הַקַּדַּחַת מְכַלּוֹת
עֵינַיִם וּמְדִיבֹת נָפֶשׁ וּזְרַעְתֶּם
לָרִיק זַרְעֲכֶם וַאֲכָלֻהוּ אֹיְבֵיכֶם

Leviticus 26:16

ＶＰＸ＋

והו (THW) Strong's #8414,8429/ AHLB #1488

A barren place

To consider of no value

Empty space

Waste place

*None calleth for justice, nor any pleadeth for truth: they trust in **vanity**, and speak lies; they conceive mischief, and bring forth iniquity.*

אֵין־קֹרֵא בְצֶדֶק וְאֵין נִשְׁפָּט
בֶּאֱמוּנָה בָּטוֹחַ עַל־**תֹּהוּ** וְדַבֶּר־שָׁוְא
הָרוֹ עָמָל וְהוֹלֵיד אָוֶן

Isaiah 59:4

צֿₘנֿ/

הבל (HBL) Strong's #1892/ AHLB #1035

Vapor
Lack value
Breath
Temporary

*They have moved me to jealousy with that which is not Elohim; they have provoked me to anger with their **vanities**[1]: and I will move them to jealousy with those which are not a people; I will provoke them to anger with a foolish nation.*

---

[1] This word is also translated as idol in other versions of scripture.

הֵם קִנְאוּנִי בְלֹא־אֵל כִּעֲסוּנִי
בְּהַבְלֵיהֶם וַאֲנִי אַקְנִיאֵם בְּלֹא־
עָם בְּגוֹי נָבָל אַכְעִיסֵם

Deuteronomy 32:21

<u>שוא</u> (ShWA) Strong's #7723/ AHLB #1461

Desolate

Destroy

Leave Empty

Thou shalt not take the name of Yahuah thy Elohim in vain; for Yahuah will not hold him guiltless that taketh his name in vain.

לֹא תִשָּׂא אֶת־שֵׁם־יְהוָה אֱלֹהֶיךָ
לַשָּׁוְא כִּי לֹא יְנַקֶּה יְהֹוָה אֵת אֲשֶׁר־
יִשָּׂא אֶת־שְׁמוֹ
לַשָּׁוְא

Exodus 20:7

Hair: Sear (שער)

His head and his hairs were white like wool, as white as snow; and his eyes were as a flame of fire;
Revelation 1:14

שער\ס (HBL) Strong's #1892/ AHLB #1035
Fearing/ dreading
Growing hair
Shine
Illuminate
Encircle
Storm cloud

*And when he polled his head, (for it was at every year's end that he polled it: because the hair was heavy on him, therefore he polled it:) he weighed the **hair** of his head at two hundred shekels after the king's weight.*

וּֽבְגַלְּחוֹ֩ אֶת־רֹאשׁ֨וֹ וְֽהָיָ֜ה מִקֵּ֣ץ
יָמִ֣ים ׀ לַיָּמִ֗ים אֲשֶׁ֣ר יְגַלֵּחַ֮ כִּֽי־כָבֵ֣ד
עָלָיו֮ וְגִלְּח֒וֹ וְשָׁקַל֙ אֶת־**שְׂעַ֣ר**
רֹאשׁ֔וֹ מָאתַ֥יִם שְׁקָלִ֖ים בְּאֶ֥בֶן
הַמֶּֽלֶךְ

2 Samuel 14:26

𐤀𐤋𐤃

דלה (DLH) Strong's #1802,1808-9 AHLB #1081

What hangs from the head
Blown in the wind
Drawing up water
High hanging branches
Raised hair (afro)

Counsel in the heart of man is like deep water;
*but a man of understanding **will draw it out**.*

מַיִם עֲמֻקִים עֵצָה בְלֶב־אִישׁ וְאִישׁ
תְּבוּנָה **יִדְלֶנָּה**²

Proverbs 20:5

𐤌𐤔𐤒

קשה (QShH) Strong's #4748/ AHLB #1435

Bunched hair
Solid piece of hair
Ensnare
Covered
Gather

---

² This word gives us an insight into the story of Samson and Delilah (same root word). She drew out the truth from Samson about his hair.

Stalk of grain with a cord wrapped around the middle

*And it shall come to pass, that instead of sweet smell there shall be stink; and instead of a girdle a rent; and instead of **well set hair** baldness; and instead of a stomacher a girding of sackcloth; and burning instead of beauty.*

וְהָיָה֩ תַּ֨חַת בֹּ֜שֶׂם מַ֣ק יִֽהְיֶ֗ה
וְתַ֨חַת חֲגוֹרָ֤ה נִקְפָּה֙ וְתַ֤חַת מַעֲשֶׂ֣ה
מִקְשֶׁה֙ קָרְחָ֔ה וְתַ֥חַת פְּתִיגִ֖יל
מַחֲגֹ֣רֶת שָׂ֑ק כִּי־תַ֖חַת יֹֽפִי

Isaiah 3:24

נֵ֣זֶר (N-ZR) Strong's #5139,5144-5/ AHLB #2390
Crown
Separation
Unattended vine
Nazarite
Dedicate
Shaved head of dedication

The blessings of thy father have prevailed above the blessings of my progenitors unto the utmost *bound of the everlasting hills: they shall be on the head of Joseph, and on the crown of the head of him that was **separate** [3]from his brethren.*

בִּרְכֹת אָבִ֔יךָ גָּבְרוּ֙ עַל־בִּרְכֹת הוֹרַ֔י
עַד־תַּאֲוַ֖ת גִּבְעֹ֣ת עוֹלָ֑ם תִּֽהְיֶ֙יןָ֙ לְרֹ֣אשׁ
יוֹסֵ֔ף
וּלְקָדְקֹ֖ד **נְזִ֥יר** אֶחָֽיו

Genesis 49:26

פרע (PRA) Strong's #6545/ AHLB #2641

Long

Lose of cut hair

Lose complete control

Wild hair

locks

*And the priest shall set the woman before Yahuah, **and uncover**[4] the woman's head, and put the offering of memorial in her hands, which is the jealousy offering: and the priest shall*

---

[3] It is possible that Joseph was set apart as a Nazarite.

[4] To cut her hair

have in his hand the bitter water that causeth the curse

וְהֶעֱמִ֨יד הַכֹּהֵ֜ן אֶת־הָאִשָּׁה֮ לִפְנֵ֣י יְהוָה֒ **וּפָרַע֙** אֶת־רֹ֣אשׁ הָֽאִשָּׁ֔ה וְנָתַ֣ן עַל־כַּפֶּ֗יהָ אֵ֚ת מִנְחַ֣ת הַזִּכָּרֹ֔ון מִנְחַ֥ת קְנָאֹ֖ת הִ֑וא וּבְיַ֣ד הַכֹּהֵ֗ן יִהְי֛וּ מֵ֥י הַמָּרִ֖ים הַמְאָֽרֲרִֽים

Numbers 5:18

Heart/Soul: Leb (לב)

לב (LBB) Strong's #3820,3823-5/ AHLB #1255
Joined at the core
Conquering the heart
Inner man
Mind
Understanding
Ego

*Then Abraham fell upon his face, and laughed, and said **in his heart**, Shall a child be born unto him that is an hundred years old? and shall Sarah, that is ninety years old, bear?*

וַיִּפֹּל אַבְרָהָם עַל־פָּנָיו וַיִּצְחָק
וַיֹּאמֶר **בְּלִבּוֹ** הַלְּבֶן מֵאָה־שָׁנָה יִוָּלֵד
וְאִם־שָׂרָה הֲבַת־תִּשְׁעִים שָׁנָה תֵּלֵד

Genesis 17:17

__נפש__ (NPhSh) Strong's #5315/ AHLB #2523
Soul giving life to the body
Determination
Living personality
What makes a person an individual
Passion
Emotion
Desire

*But he himself went a day's journey into the wilderness, and came and sat down under a juniper tree: and he requested for himself that he might die; and said, It is enough; now, O LORD, take away **my life**; for I am not better than my fathers.*

וְהֽוּא־הָלַ֤ךְ בַּמִּדְבָּר֙ דֶּ֣רֶךְ י֔וֹם
וַיָּבֹ֕א וַיֵּ֖שֶׁב תַּ֣חַת רֹ֥תֶם [אַחַת כ]
(אֶחָ֑ד ק) וַיִּשְׁאַ֤ל אֶת־נַפְשׁוֹ֙ לָמ֔וּת
וַיֹּ֣אמֶר ׀ רַ֗ב עַתָּ֤ה יְהוָה֙ קַ֣ח __נַפְשִׁ֔י__
כִּ֛י־לֹא־ט֥וֹב אָנֹכִ֖י מֵאֲבֹתָֽי׃

1 Kings 19:4

Witchcraft or Inquiring: Owb (אוב)

For rebellion is as the sin of witchcraft, and stubbornness is as iniquity and idolatry.
1 Samuel 15:23

<u>אוב</u> (AWB) Strong's #178/ AHLB #1002

Oracle invoking rain

Necromancer

Mediums

Carrying a false ones name (making someone your father)

Hallowed vessel

Allowing spirits to speak through you

Ventriloquist

*Regard not them **that have familiar spirits**, neither seek after wizards, to be defiled by them: I am Yahuah your Elohim.*

אַל־תִּפְנוּ אֶל־**הָאֹבֹת** וְאֶל־הַיִּדְּעֹנִים אַל־
תְּבַקְשׁוּ לְטָמְאָה בָהֶם אֲנִי יְהֹוָה אֱלֹהֵיכֶם

Leviticus 19:31

דרש (DRSh) Strong's #1875,4097/ AHLB #2114

Seeking

Inquiring

Demanding return of something (an answer)

Studying expounding

Investigating

Worship a deity

And the children struggled together within her; and she said, If it be so, why am I thus? And she went to **inquire** *of Yahuah.*

וַיִּתְרֹצֲצוּ הַבָּנִים בְּקִרְבָּהּ וַתֹּאמֶר
אִם־כֵּן לָמָּה זֶּה אָנֹכִי וַתֵּלֶךְ **לִדְרֹשׁ**
אֶת־יְהוָֹה

Genesis 25:22

שאל (S-AL) Strong's #7592-3/ AHLB #1472

Request movement

Demand removal
Grave demanding the return of the body
Asking
Seeking what is unknown
Desire
Draw out

*Is it not wheat harvest to day? I will call unto Yahuah, and he shall send thunder and rain; that ye may perceive and see that your wickedness is great, which ye have done in the sight of Yahuah, **in asking** you a king.*

הֲל֣וֹא קְצִיר־חִטִּים֮ הַיּוֹם֒ אֶקְרָא֙
אֶל־יְהוָ֔ה וְיִתֵּ֥ן קֹל֖וֹת וּמָטָ֑ר וּדְע֣וּ
וּרְא֗וּ כִּֽי־רָעַתְכֶ֤ם רַבָּה֙ אֲשֶׁ֣ר
עֲשִׂיתֶם֙ בְּעֵינֵ֣י יְהוָ֔ה **לִשְׁא֥וֹל** לָכֶ֖ם
מֶֽלֶךְ

1 Samuel 12:17

𐤉𐤌𐤋

הבר (HBL) Strong's #1895/ AHLB #1043
Analyze
Astrologers
Divide the stars

Eat, divide
Covenant through joint sacrifice
Join through communion

Thou art wearied in the multitude of thy counsels.
*Let now the **astrologers**, the stargazers, the*
monthly prognosticators, stand up, and save
thee from these things that shall come upon
thee.

נִלְאֵית בְּרֹב עֲצָתָיִךְ יַעַמְדוּ־נָא
וְיוֹשִׁיעֻךְ [הַבְרוּ כ] (הַבְרִי ק) שָׁמַיִם
הַחֹזִים בַּכּוֹכָבִים מוֹדִיעִם לֶחֳדָשִׁים
מֵאֲשֶׁר יָבֹאוּ עָלָיִךְ

Isaiah 47:13

עַנַן (ANN) Strong's #6050-1,6053/ AHLB #1359
Cloud
To watch
The eye
Watching over something of importance
To tell the weather/climate
Watch the clouds
Looking to the sky

*There shall not be found among you any one that maketh his son or his daughter to pass through the fire, or that useth divination, or **an observer of times**, or an enchanter, or a witch*

לֹא־יִמָּצֵא בְךָ֗ מַעֲבִ֤יר בְּנֽוֹ־וּבִתּוֹ בָּאֵ֔שׁ קֹסֵ֣ם קְסָמִ֔ים **מְעוֹנֵ֥ן** וּמְנַחֵ֖שׁ וּמְכַשֵּֽׁף

Deuteronomy 18:10

קסם (QSM) Strong's #7080-1/ AHLB #2718
Divination
Perform feat beyond comprehension
Soothsayer

*And the elders of Moab and the elders of Midian departed with the rewards of **divination** in their hand; and they came unto Balaam, and spake unto him the words of Balak.*

וַיֵּ֣לְכ֗וּ זִקְנֵ֤י מוֹאָב֙ וְזִקְנֵ֣י מִדְיָ֔ן **וּקְסָמִ֖ים** בְּיָדָ֑ם וַיָּבֹ֙אוּ֙ אֶל־בִּלְעָ֔ם וַיְדַבְּר֥וּ אֵלָ֖יו דִּבְרֵ֥י בָלָֽק

Numbers 22:7

ᏞᎥᎥᎥᏌ

<u>לחש</u> (LKhSh) <u>Strong's #3907-8/ AHLB #2308</u>
Whisper
Enchantment
Amulet to which prayers are directed

Surely the serpent will bite without
enchantment; and a babbler is no better.

אִם־יִשֹּׁךְ הַנָּחָשׁ בְּלוֹא־**לָחַשׁ** וְאֵין
יִתְרֹון לְבַעַל הַלָּשֹׁון
Ecclesiastes 10:11

<u>ידעני</u> (Ydani) <u>Strong's #3049/ AHLB #1085</u>
One with special knowledge
Familiar spirit

And he made his son pass through the fire, and
observed times, and used enchantments, and
*dealt with **familiar spirits** and wizards: he*

wrought much wickedness in the sight of Yahuah,
to provoke him to anger.

וְהֶעֱבִיר אֶת־בְּנוֹ בָּאֵשׁ וְעוֹנֵן וְנִחֵשׁ
וְעָשָׂה אוֹב **וְיִדְּעֹנִים** הִרְבָּה לַעֲשׂוֹת
הָרַע בְּעֵינֵי
יְהוָה לְהַכְעִיס

2 Kings 21:6

ᎳᎳᎢᎣᎣᎳ

כחשׁ (KhHhSh) Strong's #3584-6/ AHLB #2257

Lying
Denying
Disappointing
Deceive
Fail
Withholding or denying something which causes
leanness
Making weak or frail through a lie
Pretending

And it shall come to pass in that day, that the
prophets shall be ashamed every one of his
vision, when he hath prophesied; neither shall
*they wear a rough garment to **deceive**:*

וְהָיָה ׀ בַּיּוֹם הַהֹוּא יֵבֹשׁוּ הַנְּבִיאֶים
אִישׁ מֵחֶזְיֹנֹוֹ בְּהִנָּבְאֹתֶוֹ וְלֹא יִלְבְּשׁוּ
אַדֶּרֶת שֵׂעָר לְמַעַן **כַּחֵשׁ**

Zechariah 13:4

Follow: Dabaq (דבק)

דבק (DBQ) Strong's #1692-3 / AHLB #2092

Cleave
Reaching
Glue
Connector
Adhere
Join
Stick to someone or something

*Thou shalt fear Yahuah your Elohim; him shalt thou serve, and to him shalt thou **cleave**, and swear by his name.*

אֶת־יְהוָה אֱלֹהֶיךָ תִּירָא אֹתוֹ תַעֲבֹד
וּבוֹ **תִדְבָּק** וּבִשְׁמוֹ תִּשָּׁבֵעַ

Deuteronomy 10:20

אחר (ACHR) Strong's #310-12 / AHLB #1181

After
To Follow After
Being behind

And he said, I will certainly return unto thee
according to the time of life; and, lo, Sarah thy wife
shall have a son. And Sarah heard it in the tent door,
*which was **behind** him.*

וַיֹּאמֶר שׁוֹב אָשׁוּב אֵלֶיךָ כָּעֵת חַיָּה
וְהִנֵּה־בֵן לְשָׂרָה אִשְׁתֶּךָ וְשָׂרָה שֹׁמַעַת
פֶּתַח הָאֹהֶל וְהוּא **אַחֲרָיו**

Genesis 18:10

רגל (RGL) Strong's #7271-2/ AHLB #2749

Foot
Travel on foot/ Journey
Learn step by step
Being in accord with current activity
Walk/slander (carry information)
Able to keep up and endure

Let my lord, I pray thee, pass over before his servant:
*and I will **lead on** softly, according as the cattle that*
goeth before me and the children be able to endure,
until I come unto my lord unto Seir.

יַעֲבָר־נָא אֲדֹנִי לִפְנֵי עַבְדּוֹ וַאֲנִי
אֶתְנָהֲלָה לְאִטִּי **לְרֶגֶל** הַמְּלָאכָה אֲשֶׁר־
לְפָנַי וּלְרֶגֶל הַיְלָדִים עַד אֲשֶׁר־אָבֹא אֶל־
אֲדֹנִי שֵׂעִירָה
Genesis 33:14

רדף (RDP) Strong's #7291/ AHLB #2755

Follow
Pursue
Chase
Striving eagerly
Pursuing with justification
Hunting down
Seeking aims and objectives

And he took his brethren with him, and pursued after him seven days' journey; and they overtook him in the mount Gilead.

וַיִּקַּח אֶת־אֶחָיו עִמּוֹ וַיִּרְדֹּף אַחֲרָיו דֶּרֶךְ
שִׁבְעַת יָמִים וַיַּדְבֵּק אֹתוֹ בְּהַר הַגִּלְעָד
Genesis 31:23

STUDY THIRTY-SEVEN

Lead: Nahal (נהל)

נהל (NHL) Strong's #5095/ AHLB #1311

Flow

Move downward

Stream leading to large body of water

Drive/Guide

Lead to pasture

Continue toward the staff

*Thou in thy mercy hast led forth the
people which thou hast redeemed: thou hast
guided them in thy strength unto thy holy habitation.*

נָחִיתָ בְחַסְדְּךָ עַם־זוּ גָּאָלְתָּ **נֵהַלְתָּ**
בְעָזְּךָ אֶל־נְוֵה קָדְשֶׁךָ

Exodus 15:13

נהג (NGA) Strong's #5090/ AHLB #1302

Vocalize instruction for movement

Shout/yell
Pushing or guiding

And he carried away all his cattle, and all his goods which he had gotten, the cattle of his getting, which he had gotten in Padanaram, for to go to Isaac his father in the land of Canaan.

וַיִּנְהַג אֶת־כָּל־מִקְנֵהוּ וְאֶת־כָּל־רְכֻשׁוֹ
אֲשֶׁר רָכָשׁ מִקְנֵה קִנְיָנוֹ אֲשֶׁר רָכַשׁ בְּפַדַּן
אֲרָם לָבוֹא אֶל־יִצְחָק אָבִיו אַרְצָה כְּנָעַן

Genesis 31:18

נחה (NChH) Strong's #5148/ AHLB #1307
Satisfy
Lead to self-endorsed goal
Acceding
Satisfaction

*And he said, Blessed be Yahuah Elohim of my master Abraham, who hath not left destitute my master of his mercy and his truth: I being in the way, Yahuah **led me** to the house of my master's brethren.*

וַיֹּאמֶר בָּרוּךְ יְהוָה אֱלֹהֵי אֲדֹנִי
אַבְרָהָם אֲשֶׁר לֹא־עָזַב חַסְדּוֹ וַאֲמִתּוֹ מֵעִם
אֲדֹנִי אָנֹכִי בַּדֶּרֶךְ **נָחַנִי** יְהוָה בֵּית אֲחֵי אֲדֹנִי

Genesis 24:27

שׁאֵרִ

__דרך (DRK) Strong's #1869/ AHLB #2112

Tread
Take a step
Path of Life
Walk

*Save Caleb the son of Jephunneh; he shall see it, and
to him will I give the land that he hath trodden upon,
and to his children, because he hath wholly followed
Yahuah.*

זוּלָתִי כָּלֵב בֶּן־יְפֻנֶּה הוּא יִרְאֶנָּה וְלוֹ־
אֶתֵּן אֶת־הָאָרֶץ אֲשֶׁר **דָּרַךְ**־בָּהּ וּלְבָנָיו יַעַן
אֲשֶׁר מִלֵּא אַחֲרֵי יְהוָה:

Deuteronomy 1:36

__נגד (NGD) Strong's #5046-9, 5057/ AHLB #2373

One who tells orders

Before- to show yourself in front of another
Tell
Give an account to another

And he said, Who told thee that thou wast naked?
Hast thou eaten of the tree, whereof I commanded
thee that thou shouldest not eat?

וַיֹּ֕אמֶר **מִ֚י הִגִּ֣יד** לְךָ֔ כִּ֥י עֵירֹ֖ם אָ֑תָּה
הֲמִן־הָעֵ֗ץ אֲשֶׁ֧ר צִוִּיתִ֛יךָ לְבִלְתִּ֥י אֲכָל־מִמֶּ֖נּוּ
אָכָֽלְתָּ

Genesis 3:11

STUDY THIRTY-EIGHT

Vision: Chazah (חזה)

But ye, beloved, building up yourselves on your most holy faith, praying in the Holy Ghost,
Jude 1:20

חזה (ChZH) Strong's #2372/ AHLB #1168

Light piercing through darkness
See what is not normally visible
See from afar
foresight

*And upon the nobles of the children of Israel he laid not his hand: also they **saw** Elohim, and did eat and drink.*

וְאֶל־אֲצִילֵי בְּנֵי יִשְׂרָאֵל לֹא שָׁלַח יָדֹו
וַֽיֶּחֱזוּ אֶת־הָֽאֱלֹהִים וַיֹּאכְלוּ וַיִּשְׁתּֽוּ
Exodus 24:11

<u>ראה (RAH) Strong's #7200/ AHLB #1438</u>

Look
See and understand
Prophesying
Searching
Looking at another
Mirror
Sharp-eye Bird

And Elohim saw the light, that it was good: and God divided the light from the darkness.

וַיַּרְא אֱלֹהִים אֶת־הָאוֹר כִּי־טוֹב
וַיַּבְדֵּל אֱלֹהִים בֵּין הָאוֹר וּבֵין הַחֹשֶׁךְ
Genesis 1:4

STUDY THIRTY-NINE

Encourage: Chazaq (חזק)

But ye, beloved, building up yourselves on your most holy faith, praying in the Holy Ghost,
Jude 1:20

חזק (HhZQ) Strong's #2388,2392/ AHLB #2152
Hold tightly
Strengthen
Being courageous
Pressing toward a goal
Fastening
Seize
Prepare for battle

*But Joshua the son of Nun, which standeth before thee, he shall go in thither: **encourage** him: for he shall cause Israel to inherit it.*

יְהוֹשֻׁעַ בִּן־נוּן֩ הָעֹמֵ֨ד לְפָנֶ֜יךָ ה֣וּא יָ֣בֹא
שָׁ֗מָּה אֹת֣וֹ **חַזֵּ֔ק** כִּי־ה֖וּא יַנְחִלֶ֥נָּה אֶת־יִשְׂרָאֵֽל
Deuteronomy 1:38

Vengeance: Naqam (נקם)

Dearly beloved, avenge not yourselves, but rather give place unto wrath: for it is written, Vengeance is mine; I will repay, saith Yahuah.

Romans 12:19

<u>נקם</u> (HhZQ) Strong's #5358/ AHLB #1427,2433

Avenge

One who raises hand to another

To stand up against

*Thou shalt not **avenge,** nor bear any grudge against the children of thy people, but thou shalt love thy neighbour as thyself: I am Yahuah*

לֹא־**תִקֹּם** וְלֹא־תִטֹּר אֶת־בְּנֵי עַמֶּךָ וְאָהַבְתָּ לְרֵעֲךָ כָּמוֹךָ אֲנִי יְהוָה

Leviticus 19:18

Contentious: Madon (מדון)

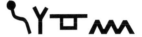

מדון (MDN) Strong's #1777,4066,4079,4090/ AHLB #1083

Sentencing

Final judgment

Defend

Dispute

Vindictive

Brawling

Rule over

Discord

It is better to dwell in a corner of the housetop, than with a brawling[5] women in a wide house.

טֹוב לָשֶׁבֶת עַל־פִּנַּת־גָּג מֵאֵשֶׁת
מְדִינִים וּבֵית חָבֶר

Proverbs 21:9

---

[5] contentious

Foolish: Lo (לוא)

לוא (LO) Strong's #191,194,196,3808,3863/ AHLB #1254

Idol
To be without
Foolish
Without wisdom

For my people *is* foolish, they have not known me; they *are* sottish children, and they have none understanding: they *are* wise to do evil, but to do good they have no knowledge.

כִּי | **אֱוִיל**⁶ עַמִּי אוֹתִי לֹא יָדָעוּ בָּנִים
סְכָלִים הֵמָּה וְלֹא נְבוֹנִים
הֵמָּה חֲכָמִים הֵמָּה לְהָרַע
וּלְהֵיטִיב **לֹא** יָדָעוּ

Jeremiah 4:22

---

⁶ One of the words for foolish in Hebrew is evil **אויל**. Look up this word in your personal study time.

יֹפֵס

נבל (NBL) Strong's #1077,1097,1099,1101,5036,8399/ AHLB #2396

Flow

To come to nothing when effort is given

Exchange

Confusion (act lacking results)

Do ye thus requite Yahuah, O **foolish** people and unwise? *is* not he thy father *that* hath bought thee? hath he not made thee, and established thee?

הֲ־לַיְהוָה֙ תִּגְמְלוּ־זֹ֔את עַ֥ם **נָבָ֖ל**
וְלֹ֣א חָכָ֑ם הֲלוֹא־הוּא֙ אָבִ֣יךָ קָּנֶ֔ךָ ה֥וּא
עָֽשְׂךָ֖ וַֽיְכֹנְנֶֽךָ

Deuteronomy 32:6

עשֵׁל

כסל (CSL) Strong's #3684,3688,5528/ AHLB #2275

Loins

Confidence

Confidence in something foolish

Folly

Boasting in your loins

Understand, ye brutish among the people: and *ye* **fools**, when will ye be wise?

בִּינוּ בֹּעֲרִים בָּעָם **וּכְסִילִים** מָתַי תַּשְׂכִּילוּ

Psalm 94:8

פתי (PTY) Strong's #6612/ AHLB #1390

Gullible
Seducing
Responding to outside influences
Place of debauchery
Full of wholes
A hole for intercourse
Inexperienced

The **simple** believeth every word: but the prudent *man* looketh well to his going.

פֶּתִי יַאֲמִין לְכָל־דָּבָר וְעָרוּם יָבִין לַאֲשֻׁרוֹ

Proverbs 14:15

<u>בער</u> (BER) Strong's #1198/ AHLB #2028

Senseless

Brutish

Burn

Kindle fire

So **_foolish_** _was I, and ignorant: I was as a beast before thee._

וַאֲנִי־**בַעַר** וְלֹא אֵדָע בְּהֵמוֹת הָיִיתִי
עִמָּךְ

Psalm 73:22

<u>תפל</u> (TPL) Strong's #8602,8604 AHLB #2898

Tasteless

Untampered

Foolish

Folly

Worthless

*Thy prophets have seen vain and __foolish__ things
for thee: and they have not discovered thine
iniquity, to turn away thy captivity; but have seen
for thee false burdens and causes of
banishment.*

נְבִיאַ֗יִךְ חָ֤זוּ לָךְ֙ שָׁ֣וְא **וְתָפֵ֔ל** וְלֹֽא־
גִלּ֥וּ עַל־עֲוֺנֵ֖ךְ לְהָשִׁ֣יב [שְׁבִיתֵ֑ךְ כ]
(שְׁבוּתֵ֑ךְ ק)
וַיֶּחֱזוּ לָ֔ךְ מַשְׂא֥וֹת שָׁ֖וְא וּמַדּוּחִֽים

Lamentations 2:14

Bridegroom: Chatan (חתן)

חתן (HhTN) Strong's #2860 AHLB #2224

Tie together for mutual satisfaction

Delightful family relations

Relate

Infant at circumcision

Wedding

Relationship through marriage

*Which is as a **bridegroom** coming out of his*
chamber, and rejoiceth as a strong man to run a race.

וְהֹוּא **כְּחָתָן** יֵצֵא מֵחֻפָּתֹו יָשֵׂישׂ כְּגִבֹּור
לָרוּץ אֹרַח

Psalm 19:5

Bride/Wife: Kallah (כלה)

An excellent wife is the crown of her husband, But she who shames him is like rottenness in his bones.
Proverbs 12:4

ע‍‍‍ل‍‍‍ל

כלל (KLL) Strong's #3618,3623,3623,3634-5,4359/ AHLB #1242

The choice piece

Perfection

Vessel

Consummation

Tame for the yoke

A container for holding contents

Bride (one who makes man complete)

Out of Zion, the **perfection** of beauty, Elohim hath shined..

מִצִּיּוֹן **מִכְלַל**־יֹפִי אֱלֹהִים הוֹפִיעַ

Psalm 50:2

ⳑ⊙⊡

בעל (BAL) Strong's #1166-7,1169/ AHLB #2027

Dominion

Owning

Rule

Marrying

Having a husband

Head of

Wooing

Mastering

Possession

Idolatry

Bind/yoke

Thou shalt no more be termed Forsaken; neither shall thy land any more be termed Desolate: but thou shalt be called Hephzibah, and thy land **Beulah***: for Yahuah delighteth in thee, and thy land shall be married.*

לֹא־יֵאָמֵר֩ לָ֨ךְ ע֜וֹד עֲזוּבָ֗ה וּלְאַרְצֵךְ֙
לֹא־יֵאָמֵ֥ר עוֹד֙ שְׁמָמָ֔ה כִּ֣י לָ֗ךְ יִקָּרֵ֤א
חֶפְצִי־בָהּ֙ וּלְאַרְצֵ֣ךְ **בְּעוּלָ֔ה** כִּֽי־חָפֵ֤ץ
יְהוָה֙ בָּ֔ךְ וְאַרְצֵ֖ךְ תִּבָּעֵֽל

Isaiah 62:4

רעה (R-AH) Strong's #7453,7464,7468/ AHLB #1453

Tend

Satisfy needs

Lead to pasture

Being concerned

Thinking about

Seeking spiritual sustenance

Friend

Unified nation

Shepherd

Purpose

Aim

Desire

Man watches

Female companion

*Thou knowest my downsitting and mine uprising, thou understandest **my thought** afar off.*

אַתָּה יָדַעְתָּ שִׁבְתִּי וְקוּמִי בַּנְתָּה
לְרֵעִי מֵרָחוֹק

Psalm 139:2

חתן (HhTN) Strong's #2859,2860-1/ AHLB #2224

Relate

Tie together for mutual satisfaction

Delightful relations

Wedding

Son in law

Infant at circumcision

Circumciser

To take hold of

A daughter's husband

Bridegroom

Mother-in-law

Neither shalt thou make marriages with them; thy daughter thou shalt not give unto his son, nor his daughter shalt thou take unto thy son.

וְלֹא תִתְחַתֵּן בָּם בִּתְּךָ לֹא־תִתֵּן לִבְנֹו וּבִתֹּו לֹא־תִקַּח לִבְנֶךָ

Deuteronomy 7:3

Menstruation: Niddah (נדה)

Classification of menstrual cycle phase

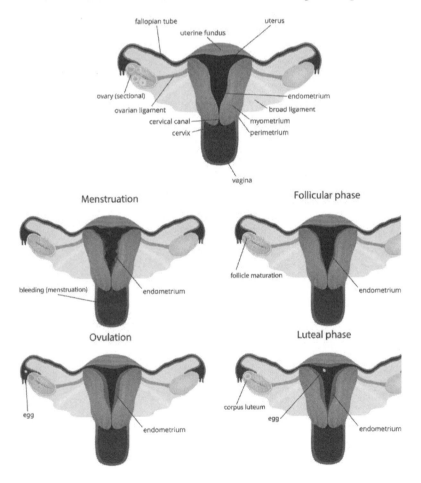

נדה <u>(NDH) Strong's #5079,5206/ AHLB #1303</u>

Removal

Toss out

Cloth

Cut away

Distance due to impurity

Separation

*And if a woman have an issue, and her issue in her flesh be blood, she shall be **put apart** seven days: and whosoever toucheth her shall be unclean until the even.*

וְאִשָּׁה֙ כִּי־תִהְיֶ֣ה זָבָ֔ה דָּ֛ם יִהְיֶ֥ה זֹבָ֖הּ בִּבְשָׂרָ֑הּ שִׁבְעַ֤ת יָמִים֙ תִּהְיֶ֣ה **בְנִדָּתָ֔הּ** וְכָל־

הַנֹּגֵ֥עַ בָּ֖הּ יִטְמָ֥א עַד־הָעָֽרֶב

Leviticus 15:19

Uncleanliness: Tame (טמא)

טמא <u>(ThM) Strong's #2930/ AHLB #1197</u>

Consummate

Lose purity

Defile

Lose freedom

To shut

To bind to

*Regard not them that have familiar spirits, neither seek after wizards, to be **defiled** by them: I am Yahuah your Elohim.*

אַל־תִּפְנ֤וּ אֶל־הָאֹבֹת֙ וְאֶל־הַיִּדְּעֹנִ֔ים
אַל־ תְּבַקְשׁ֖וּ **לְטָמְאָ֣ה** בָהֶ֑ם אֲנִ֖י
יְהוָ֥ה אֱלֹהֵיכֶֽם

Leviticus 19:31

עַרה <u>(AhRH) Strong's #6168,6196/ AHLB #1365</u>

Bare

Absorb impressions

Empty

Uncovering

Exposing

Being naked

Make sensitive

Destroy a protected place

*And if a man shall lie with a woman having her sickness, and shall uncover her nakedness; he **<u>hath discovered</u>** her fountain, and she hath uncovered the fountain of her blood: and both of them shall be cut off from among their people.*

וְאִישׁ אֲשֶׁר־יִשְׁכַּב אֶת־אִשָּׁה דָּוָה
וְגִלָּה אֶת־עֶרְוָתָהּ אֶת־מְקֹרָהּ
הֶעֱרָה וְהִיא גִּלְּתָה אֶת־מְקוֹר
דָּמֶיהָ וְנִכְרְתוּ שְׁנֵיהֶם מִקֶּרֶב עַמָּם
Leviticus 20:18

Marriage: Eden (עדן)

עדן (EDN) Strong's #5727,5730/ AHLB #2528

Satisfy all needs

Delight

Give joy

Expensive shackles

Fancy food

Pleasure

Delicate

Luxurious

Therefore Sarah laughed within herself, saying, After I am waxed old shall I **have pleasure**, my lord being old also?

וַתִּצְחַק שָׂרָה בְּקִרְבָּהּ לֵאמֹר
אַחֲרֵי בְלֹתִי הָיְתָה־לִּי **עֶדְנָה**
וַאדֹנִי זָקֵן

Genesis 18:12

עטר (ATR) Strong's #5849,5850/ AHLB #2538

Delicate
Breast
Sustain
Being wrapped up in
To become the authority over

Go forth, O ye daughters of Zion, and behold king Solomon with the **crown** wherewith his mother crowned him in the day of his espousals, and in the day of the gladness of his heart.

צְאֶינָה ׀ וּרְאֶינָה בְּנוֹת צִיּוֹן בַּמֶּלֶךְ שְׁלֹמֹה **בָּעֲטָרָה** שֶׁעִטְּרָה־לּוֹ אִמּוֹ בְּיוֹם חֲתֻנָּתוֹ וּבְיוֹם שִׂמְחַת לִבּוֹ

Song of Solomon 3:11

STUDY FORTY-EIGHT

Obey: Shama (שמע)

O earth, earth, earth, hear the word of the LORD.
Jeremiah 22:29

שמע (ShMA) Strong's #5561,8033-4,8035-6/ AHLB #1473

Listening

Obey

Responding and doing

Action evoked by authority

Reciprocity because of position and worth

Now therefore **hearken**, O Israel, unto the statutes and unto the judgments, which I teach you, for to do *them*, that ye may live, and go in and possess the land which Yahuah Elohim of your fathers giveth you.

וְעַתָּה יִשְׂרָאֵל **שְׁמַע** אֶל־הֶחֻקִּים

וְאֶל־הַמִּשְׁפָּטִים אֲשֶׁר אָנֹכִי מְלַמֵּד
אֶתְכֶם לַעֲשֹׂות לְמַעַן תִּחְיוּ וּבָאתֶם
וִירִשְׁתֶּם
אֶת־הָאָרֶץ אֲשֶׁר יְהֹוָה אֱלֹהֵי אֲבֹתֵיכֶם
נֹתֵן לָכֶם

Deuteronomy 4:1

ᎷᏞᏞ

שֵׁם (ShM) Strong's #8034/ AHLB #1473

Character or fame of a person
Name
What makes one worthy
Sweet aroma that is carried
Breath

O give thanks unto Yahuah; call upon **his name**:
make known his deeds among the people.

הֹודוּ לַיהֹוָה קִרְאוּ **בִשְׁמֹו** הֹודִיעוּ
בָעַמִּים עֲלִילֹותָיו

Psalm 105:1

ש◉⚇

שעה (ShAH) Strong's #8159,8160/ AHLB #1476

Delight

Caring for with delight

Looking out for danger

Destroy the enemy

Object of constant care

Turning in acceptance

I will delight myself in thy statutes: I will not forget thy word.

בְּחֻקֹּתֶיךָ **אֶשְׁתַּעֲשָׁע** לֹא אֶשְׁכַּח דְּבָרֶךָ

Psalm 119:16

Stronghold or Fortress: Tsud (צוד)

צוד (TsWD) Strong's #6718/ AHLB #1395

Lie down to sleep

Ambush

Fortress

Save for

Vulnerable side

Trap

Catch

Hunt

Game

Provision

Positive:

I will say of Yahuah, *He is* my refuge and my fortress: my Elohim; in him will I trust.

אֹמַר לַיהוָה מַחְסִי וּמְצוּדָתִי אֱלֹהַי
אֶבְטַח־בּֽוֹ

Psalm 91:2

Negative:

My net also will I spread upon him, and he shall
be taken in my snare: and I will bring him to
Babylon *to* the land of the Chaldeans; yet shall
he not see it, though he shall die there.

וּפָרַשְׂתִּי אֶת־רִשְׁתִּי עָלָיו וְנִתְפַּשׂ
בִּמְצוּדָתִי וְהֵבֵאתִי אֹתוֹ בָבֶלָה אֶרֶץ
כַּשְׂדִּים וְאוֹתָהּ לֹא־יִרְאֶה וְשָׁם יָמֽוּת

Ezekiel 12:13

<u>צַיִד</u> (TsYD) Strong's #3684,3688,5528/ AHLB #2275

Meat

Hunt

Game

The product of the hunt

Positive:

I will abundantly bless her provision: I will
satisfy her poor with bread.

צֵידָהּ בָּרֵךְ אֲבָרֵךְ אֶבְיוֹנֶיהָ אַשְׂבִּיעַ
לָחֶם

Psalm 132:15

Negative:

He was a mighty hunter before Yahuah:
wherefore it is said, Even as Nimrod the mighty
hunter before Yahuah.

ב הוּא־הָיָה גִבֹּר־צַיִד לִפְנֵי יְהוָה
עַל־כֵּן יֵאָמַר כְּנִמְרֹד גִּבּוֹר צַיִד
לִפְנֵי יְהוָה

Genesis 10:9

פחה (PKhH) Strong's #6341 AHLB #1376

Calamities

Plots

Traps

Rule

Govern

Put out fire

Positive:

The wicked have laid a snare for me: yet I erred not from thy precepts.

נָתְנ֬וּ רְשָׁעִ֣ים פַּ֣ח לִ֑י וּ֝מִפִּקּוּדֶ֗יךָ לֹ֣א
תָעִֽיתִי

Psalm 119:110

Negative:

Know for a certainty that Yahuah your Elohim will no more drive out *any of* these nations from before you; but they shall be snares and traps unto you, and scourges in your sides, and thorns in your eyes, until ye perish from off this good land which Yahuah your Elohim hath given you.

יָד֙וֹעַ֙ תֵּֽדְע֔וּ כִּי֩ לֹ֨א יוֹסִ֜יף יְהֹוָ֣ה
אֱלֹהֵיכֶ֗ם לְהוֹרִ֛ישׁ אֶת־הַגּוֹיִ֥ם
הָאֵ֖לֶּה מִלִּפְנֵיכֶ֑ם וְהָי֨וּ לָכֶ֜ם לְפַ֣ח
וּלְמוֹקֵ֗שׁ וּלְשֹׁטֵ֤ט
בְּצִדֵּיכֶם֙ וְלִצְנִנִ֣ים בְּעֵינֵיכֶ֔ם עַד־
אֲבׇדְכֶ֗ם מֵעַ֨ל הָאֲדָמָ֤ה הַטּוֹבָה֙
הַזֹּ֔את אֲשֶׁר֙ נָתַ֣ן
לָכֶ֔ם יְהֹוָ֖ה אֱלֹהֵיכֶֽם

Joshua 23:13

צדה (TsDH) Strong's #6658/ AHLB #1395

Target
Directing Destruction
Lay down
Ambush
Destroy

Positive:

And if a man lie not in wait, but Elohim
deliver *him* into his hand; then I will appoint
thee a place whither he shall flee.

וַאֲשֶׁר֙ לֹ֣א צָדָ֔ה וְהָאֱלֹהִ֖ים אִנָּ֣ה
לְיָד֑וֹ וְשַׂמְתִּ֤י לְךָ֙ מָק֔וֹם אֲשֶׁ֥ר יָנ֖וּס
שָֽׁמָּה

Exodus 21:13

Negative:

Moreover, my father, see, yea, see the skirt of
thy robe in my hand: for in that I cut off the skirt
of thy robe, and killed thee not, know thou and
see that *there is* neither evil nor transgression in
mine hand, and I have not sinned against thee;
yet thou huntest my soul to take it.

וְאָבִי רְאֵה גַּם רְאֵה אֶת־כְּנַף
מְעִילְךָ בְּיָדִי כִּי בְכָרְתִי אֶת־כְּנַף
מְעִילְךָ וְלֹא הֲרַגְתִּיךָ דַּע וּרְאֵה כִּי
אֵין בְּיָדִי רָעָה וָפֶשַׁע
וְלֹא־חָטָאתִי לָךְ וְאַתָּה צֹדֶה אֶת־
נַפְשִׁי
לְקַחְתָּהּ

1 Samuel 24:11

יָצַר (YTsR) Strong's #3335/ AHLB #2028

Senseless

Brutish

Burn

Kindle fire

Positive:

And Yahuah Elohim formed man *of* the dust of
the ground, and breathed into his nostrils the
breath of life; and man became a living soul.

וַיִּיצֶר יְהֹוָה אֱלֹהִים אֶת־הָאָדָם
עָפָר מִן־הָאֲדָמָה וַיִּפַּח בְּאַפָּיו

נִשְׁמַת חַיִּים וַיְהִי הָאָדָם לְנֶפֶשׁ
חַיָּה

Genesis 2:7

Negative:

Then Jacob was greatly afraid and
distressed: and he divided the people
that *was* with him, and the flocks, and
herds, and the camels, into two bands;

וַיִּירָא יַעֲקֹב מְאֹד וַיֵּצֶר לוֹ וַיַּחַץ אֶת־
הָעָם אֲשֶׁר־אִתּוֹ וְאֶת־הַצֹּאן וְאֶת־
הַבָּקָר וְהַגְּמַלִּים לִשְׁנֵי מַחֲנוֹת

Genesis 32:7

Sex: Yada (ידע)

ידע (YDA) Strong's #3045/ AHLB #1085
Knowing the difference between
Bringing to senses
Awakening
The door of the body is the eye
Window to the soul
Intimate relationship

And Adam **knew** Eve his wife; and she conceived, and bare Cain, and said, I have gotten a man from Yahuah.

וְהָאָדָם **יָדַע** אֶת־חַוָּה אִשְׁתּוֹ וַתַּהַר
וַתֵּלֶד אֶת־קַיִן וַתֹּאמֶר קָנִיתִי אִישׁ
אֶת־יְהוָה

Genesis 4:1

בוא (BWA) Strong's #935,3997/ AHLB #1024

To fill a void
Empty space
To fill a space by entering
Fulfill a desire
To increase produce
A place of entering
A gate or passage

And it came to pass in the evening, that he took Leah his daughter, and brought her to him; and he went in unto her.

וַיְהִי בָעֶרֶב וַיִּקַּח אֶת־לֵאָה בִתּוֹ
וַיָּבֵא אֹתָהּ אֵלָיו **וַיָּבֹא** אֵלֶיהָ
Genesis 29:23

שׁגה

שׁגה (ShGH) Strong's #7686/ AHLB #1463

Be ravished
To go astray
Double burden

Do it again
Err

Let her be as the loving hind and pleasant roe;
let her breasts satisfy thee at all times; and be
thou **_ravished_** *always with her love.*

אַיֶּלֶת אֲהָבִים וְיַעֲלַת־חֵן דַּדֶּיהָ
יְרַוֻּךָ בְכָל־עֵת בְּאַהֲבָתָהּ **תִּשְׁגֶּה**
תָמִיד

Proverbs 5:19

שכב

שכב (ShKhB) Strong's #7901-3/ AHLB #2834
Lay down to copulate
Sex
To lay captive

And if a man **entice** a maid that is not betrothed,
and lie with her, he shall surely endow her to be
his wife

וְכִי־**יְפַתֶּה** אִישׁ בְּתוּלָה אֲשֶׁר לֹא־
אֹרָשָׂה וְשָׁכַב עִמָּהּ מָהֹר יִמְהָרֶנָּה
לוֹ לְאִשָּׁה

Exodus 22:16

STUDY FIFTY-ONE

Covenant: Nakar (נכר)

נכר (NKhR) Strong's #5234/ AHLB #2406

Isolate

Recognize individually

Respect

Discern

Pay attention to

Acknowledge

Care for someone or something

To know something you didn't know before

*And her mother in law said unto her, Where hast thou gleaned to day? and where wroughtest thou? blessed be **he that did take knowledge** of thee. And she shewed her mother in law with whom she had wrought, and said, The man's name with whom I wrought to day is Boaz.*

וַתֹּאמֶר֩ לָ֨הּ חֲמוֹתָ֜הּ אֵיפֹ֨ה לִקַּ֤טְתְּ
הַיּוֹם֙ וְאָ֣נָה עָשִׂ֔ית יְהִ֥י **מַכִּירֵ֖ךְ** בָּר֑וּךְ
וַתַּגֵּ֣ד לַחֲמוֹתָ֗הּ אֵ֤ת אֲשֶׁר־עָשְׂתָה֙
עִמּ֔וֹ וַתֹּ֗אמֶר שֵׁ֤ם הָאִישׁ֙ אֲשֶׁ֨ר
עָשִׂ֧יתִי עִמּ֛וֹ הַיּ֖וֹם בֹּֽעַז

Ruth 2:19

ברת (BRT) Strong's #1267,1285/ AHLB #1043

Rejuvenate
Eat a meal
Feeding
Separate out parts
Choicest
Confederacy

*And he was there with Yahuah forty days and forty nights; he did neither eat bread, nor drink water. And he wrote upon the tables the words of the **covenant**, the ten commandments.*

וַֽיְהִי־שָׁ֣ם עִם־יְהוָ֗ה אַרְבָּעִ֥ים יוֹם֙
וְאַרְבָּעִ֣ים לַ֔יְלָה לֶ֚חֶם לֹ֣א אָכַ֔ל

וּמַ֖יִם לֹ֣א שָׁתָ֑ה וַיִּכְתֹּ֣ב עַל־הַלֻּחֹ֗ת
אֵ֚ת דִּבְרֵ֣י **הַבְּרִ֔ית** עֲשֶׂ֖רֶת הַדְּבָרִֽים

Exodus 34:28

שׁＲＴ

<u>כרת</u> (KhRT) Strong's #3772/ AHLB #2291

Cut off

Separating

Cutting an animal to join

*And they said, We saw certainly that the LORD
was with thee: and we said, Let there be now an
oath betwixt us, even betwixt us and thee,* **and
let us make** *a covenant with thee;*

וַיֹּאמְר֗וּ רָא֣וֹ רָאִ֙ינוּ֙ כִּי־הָיָ֤ה יְהוָה֙ |
עִמָּ֔ךְ וַנֹּ֕אמֶר תְּהִ֨י נָ֥א אָלָ֛ה בֵּינוֹתֵ֖ינוּ
בֵּינֵ֣ינוּ וּבֵינֶ֑ךָ **וְנִכְרְתָ֥ה** בְרִ֖ית עִמָּֽךְ

Genesis 26:28

<u>ידע</u> (YDA) Strong's #3045/ AHLB #1085

Knowing the difference between

Bringing to senses
Awakening
The door of the body is the eye
Window to the soul
Intimate relationship

*And Adam **knew** Eve his wife; and she conceived, and bare Cain, and said, I have gotten a man from the LORD.*

וְהָ֣אָדָ֔ם **יָדַ֖ע** אֶת־חַוָּ֣ה אִשְׁתּ֑וֹ
וַתַּ֙הַר֙ וַתֵּ֣לֶד אֶת־קַ֔יִן וַתֹּ֕אמֶר
קָנִ֥יתִי אִ֖ישׁ אֶת־יְהֹוָֽה

Genesis 4:1

Divorce: Karath (כרת)

Yahusha answered, "It was because of your hardness of heart that Moses permitted you to divorce your wives; but it was not this way from the beginning.
Matthew 19:8

שׁרֹאָ+

כרת (KhRT) Strong's #3748,3772/ AHLB #2291

Cut off

Separating

Cutting the covenant

Cut short

Cutting off from the family tree

Cut off from the husband

And I will give the men that have transgressed my covenant, which have not performed the words of the covenant which they had made before me, when they **cut** the calf in twain, and passed between the parts thereof,

וְנָתַתִּי אֶת־הָאֲנָשִׁים הָעֹבְרִים אֶת־
בְּרִתִי אֲשֶׁר לֹא־הֵקִימוּ אֶת־דִּבְרֵי
הַבְּרִית אֲשֶׁר **כָּרְתוּ** לְפָנֵי הָעֵגֶל
אֲשֶׁר **כָּרְתוּ** לִשְׁנַיִם וַיַּעַבְרוּ בֵּין
בְּתָרָיו

Jeremiah 34:18

◼◼⸜ⵡ◼◼

שלח (ShLKh) Strong's #7971-3/ AHLB #2842

Send

Move to a goal

Abandoning of people

Allowing something to move

Move in balanced way

For Yahuah, the Elohim of Israel, saith that he hateth **putting away**: for one covereth violence with his garment, saith Yahuah of hosts: therefore take heed to your spirit, that ye deal not treacherously.

כִּי־שָׂנֵא שַׁלַּח אָמַר יְהוָה אֱלֹהֵי
יִשְׂרָאֵל וְכִסָּה חָמָס עַל־לְבוּשׁוֹ
אָמַר יְהוָה צְבָאוֹת וְנִשְׁמַרְתֶּם

בְּרוּחֲכֶם וְלֹא תִבְגֹּדוּ

Malachi 2:16

שׁאֵר

גרש (GRSh) Strong's #1645-6AHLB #2089

Send out to pasture

Eviction

Expel

Put out

Divorce

Put outside the city

Dismiss

They shall not take a wife that is a whore, or profane; neither shall they take a woman **put away** from her husband: for he is holy unto his Elohim.

אִשָּׁה זֹנָה וַחֲלָלָהֹ לֹא יִקָּחוּ וְאִשָּׁה גְרוּשָׁה מֵאִישָׁהּ לֹא יִקָּחוּ כִּי־קָדֹשׁ הוּא לֵאלֹהָיו

Leviticus 21:7

Adultery/Fornication: Zanah (זנה)

<u>נאף</u> (NAPh) Strong's #5003-4/ AHLB #2406

Heated passion

Heavy breathing

Flared Nostrils

Break wedlock

Commit adultery

Turn from one to another

And the man that committeth **adultery** *with another man's wife, even he that committeth adultery with his neighbour's wife, the adulterer and the adulteress shall surely be put to death.*

וְאִישׁ אֲשֶׁר **יִנְאַף** אֶת־אֵשֶׁת אִישׁ אֲשֶׁר יִנְאַף אֶת־אֵשֶׁת רֵעֵהוּ מוֹת־

יוּמַת הַנֹּאֵף וְהַנֹּאָפֶת

Leviticus 20:10

<u>זנה</u> (ZNH) Strong's #2181,2183-4,8457/ AHLB #1152

Whoredom

Defect

Be unfaithful

Straying

Prostituting

Forsake

Harlot

To be spread around

Literally a mattock or a hoe

A tool for cutting or tearing something apart

*Lest thou make a covenant with the inhabitants of the land, and they go a **<u>whoring</u>** after their Elohims, and do sacrifice unto their Elohims, and one call thee, and thou eat of his sacrifice;.*

פֶּן־תִּכְרֹת בְּרִית לְיוֹשֵׁב הָאָרֶץ
<u>**וְזָנוּ**</u> ׀ אַחֲרֵי אֱלֹהֵיהֶם וְזָבְחוּ
לֵאלֹהֵיהֶם וְקָרָא לְךָ וְאָכַלְתָּ
מִזִּבְחוֹ

Exodus 34:15

ᛚᚒᚦ-ᚋ-

קדש (QDSh) Strong's #6942,6948/ AHLB #2700
Whore
Set apart for special function
Separating and joining to something
Reserving and prohibiting from further use
Making independent
Being immoral

*Then he asked the men of that place, saying, Where is the harlot, that was openly by the way side? And they said, There was no **harlot** in this place.*

וַיִּשְׁאַ֞ל אֶת־אַנְשֵׁ֤י מְקֹמָהּ֙ לֵאמֹ֔ר
אַיֵּ֧ה הַקְּדֵשָׁ֛ה הִ֖וא בָעֵינַ֣יִם עַל־
הַדָּ֑רֶךְ וַיֹּ֣אמְר֔וּ לֹא־הָיְתָ֥ה בָזֶ֖ה
קדשה

Genesis 38:21

Covering: Kasah (כסה)

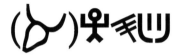

כסה/א (CSH) Strong's #3678,3677/ AHLB #1245

Throne

Seat of Authority

Cover

Conceal a person

Withdraw from sight

Elevated seat

Armor (Scales)

A mark or sign upon a person as protection

Amulet

Separate

Designated time

Allocate

Thou shalt be over my house, and according unto thy word shall all my people be ruled: only in the throne will I be greater than thou.

אַתָּה֙ תִּהְיֶ֣ה עַל־בֵּיתִ֔י וְעַל־פִּ֖יךָ
יִשַּׁ֣ק כָּל־עַמִּ֑י רַ֥ק הַכִּסֵּ֖א אֶגְדַּ֥ל מִמֶּֽךָּ

Genesis 41:40

לאט <u>(LAT) Strong's #3813/ AHLB #1262</u>

Cover

Veil

Secret

Hide the face of woman

Enchant secretly

Authority contained

Camouflaging

Wrap

But the king **covered** his face, and the king cried with a loud voice, O my son Absalom, O Absalom, my son, my son!

וְהַמֶּ֙לֶךְ֙ **לָאַ֣ט** אֶת־פָּנָ֔יו וַיִּזְעַ֥ק
הַמֶּ֛לֶךְ ק֥וֹל גָּד֖וֹל בְּנִ֣י אַבְשָׁל֑וֹם
אַבְשָׁל֖וֹם בְּנִ֥י בְנִֽי

2 Samuel 19:4

כפר (CPhR) Strong's #3722/ AHLB #2283

Protect or correct wrong

Reconcile

Forgiveness

Purge

Appease

Pardon

Cover

Atonement

Covering for a debt

Iniquities prevail against me: *as* *for* our transgressions, thou **shalt purge them away**.

דִּבְרֵי עֲוֹנֹת גָּבְרוּ מֶנִּי פְּשָׁעֵינוּ אַתָּה
תְכַפְּרֵם
Psalm 65:3

ס/שלם (SLM) Strong's #8008/ AHLB #2483

Garment (covering)

Restitution

Thy lips, O *my* spouse, drop *as* the honeycomb: honey and milk *are* under thy tongue; and the

smell of thy **<u>garments</u>** *is* like the smell of
Lebanon.

נֹפֶת תִּטֹּפְנָה שִׂפְתוֹתַיִךְ כַּלָּה
דְּבַשׁ וְחָלָב תַּחַת לְשׁוֹנֵךְ וְרֵיחַ
<u>שַׂלְמֹתַיִךְ</u> כְּרֵיחַ לְבָנוֹן
Song of Solomon 4:11

Work: Abad (עבד)

עבד (ABD) Strong's #5647-52/ AHLB #2518

Profession

Bondage/ Being a slave

Perform out of obligation

Requirement

Temple service

Provide service

Subject to another's will

Directing energies to another's goal

Constrain by external force

Servant

Go therefore now, and **work**; *for there shall no straw be given you, yet shall ye deliver the tale of bricks.*

וְעַתָּה֙ לְכ֣וּ **עִבְד֔וּ** וְתֶ֖בֶן לֹא־יִנָּתֵ֣ן לָכֶ֑ם
וְתֹ֥כֶן לְבֵנִ֖ים תִּתֵּֽנּוּ

Exodus 5:18

𐤉𐤂𐤏

יגע (YGA) Strong's #3021/ AHLB #1062

Work that brings about heavy breathing and weariness
Gasp for air
Tire
Exert oneself

Labour not to be rich: cease from thine own wisdom.

Proverbs 23:4

𐤏𐤔𐤄

עש/סה (ASH) Strong's #6213/ AHLB #1360

Doing something that causes increase
Make
Create
Forming
Causing to grow

*But the seventh day is the sabbath of Yahuah thy Elohim: in it thou shalt not do any **work**, thou, nor thy son, nor thy daughter, nor thy manservant, nor thy maidservant, nor thine ox,* *nor thine ass, nor any of thy cattle, nor thy stranger that is within thy gates; that thy manservant and thy maidservant may rest as well as thou. And remember that thou wast a servant in the land of Egypt, and that Yahuah thy Elohim brought thee out thence through a mighty hand and by a stretched out arm: therefore Yahuah thy Elohim commanded thee to keep the sabbath day.*

וְי֨וֹם הַשְּׁבִיעִ֜י שַׁבָּ֣ת ׀ לַיהֹוָ֣ה אֱלֹהֶ֗יךָ
לֹ֣א **תַעֲשֶׂ֣ה** כָל־מְלָאכָ֡ה אַתָּ֣ה וּבִנְךָ־
וּבִתֶּ֣ךָ וְעַבְדְּךָ֩ וַֽאֲמָתֶ֨ךָ וְשׁוֹרְךָ֜ וַֽחֲמֹֽרְךָ֗
וְכָל־ בְּהֶמְתֶּ֔ךָ וְגֵרְךָ֖ אֲשֶׁ֣ר בִּשְׁעָרֶ֑יךָ
לְמַ֗עַן
יָנ֛וּחַ עַבְדְּךָ֥ וַֽאֲמָֽתְךָ֖ כָּמ֑וֹךָ וְזָֽכַרְתָּ֞ כִּ֣
י־עֶ֣בֶד הָיִ֣יתָ ׀ בְּאֶ֣רֶץ מִצְרַ֗יִם וַיֹּצִ֨אֲךָ֜
יְהֹוָ֤ה אֱלֹהֶ֨יךָ֙ מִשָּׁ֔ם בְּיָ֥ד חֲזָקָ֖ה
וּבִזְרֹ֣עַ נְטוּיָ֑ה עַל־כֵּ֗ן צִוְּךָ֙ יְהֹוָ֣ה
אֱלֹהֶ֔יךָ לַֽעֲשׂ֖וֹת אֶת־ י֥וֹם הַשַּׁבָּֽת
Deuteronomy 5:14-15

עשׁ / לאשׁ

לך/לאך (LAKh) Strong's #4399/ AHLB #1264

Walk

Message

Defend Against

Serve

Work which completes a goal

Six days shall work be done: but the seventh day is the sabbath of rest, an holy convocation; ye shall do no work therein: it is the sabbath of Yahuah in all your dwellings.

וְ שֵׁ֣שֶׁת יָמִים֮ תֵּעָשֶׂה֮ **מְלָאכָה֒** וּבַיֹּ֣ום הַשְּׁבִיעִ֗י שַׁבַּ֤ת שַׁבָּתֹון֙ מִקְרָא־ קֹ֔דֶשׁ כָּל־מְלָאכָ֖ה לֹ֣א תַעֲשֹׂ֑ו שַׁבָּ֥ת הִ֛וא לַיהוָ֖ה בְּכֹ֖ל מֹושְׁבֹתֵיכֶֽם

Leviticus 23:3

על/עלל

על/עלל (ELL) Strong's #5953/ AHLB #1357

Abuse

Work

Yoke

Experience the staff
Fruit developing
Working over another
Work performed without consideration
Leading to a goal
Developing child

*And that thou mayest tell in the ears of thy son,
and of thy son's son, what things I have **wrought**
in Egypt, and my signs which I have done among
them; that ye may know how that I am Yahuah.*

וּלְמַ֡עַן תְּסַפֵּר֩ בְּאָזְנֵ֨י בִנְךָ֜ וּבֶן־בִּנְךָ֗
אֵ֣ת אֲשֶׁ֤ר **הִתְעַלַּ֨לְתִּי֙** בְּמִצְרַ֔יִם וְאֶת־
אֹתֹתַ֖י אֲשֶׁר־שַׂ֣מְתִּי בָ֑ם וִֽידַעְתֶּ֖ם כִּ֥י
אֲנִ֥י יְהוָֽה
Exodus 10:2

פעל <u>(PAL) Strong's #6466-8/ AHLB #2622</u>
Work hard to a goal
Laboring
Creating
Deeds
Do
Perform

Give them according to their deeds, and according to the wickedness of their endeavours: give them after the work of their hands; render to them their desert.

יְשַׁלֵּם יְהוָה פָּעֳלֵךְ וּתְהִי מַשְׂכֻּרְתֵּךְ שְׁלֵמָה מֵעִם יְהוָה אֱלֹהֵי יִשְׂרָאֵל אֲשֶׁר־בָּאת לַחֲסוֹת תַּחַת־כְּנָפָיו

Psalm 28:4

יצר (YTsR) Strong's #3335, 3336/ AHLB #1411

A pressing
A burden
Forming something
Pressing thought
Purpose
Intent
Planning

*The smith with the tongs both worketh in the coals, and **fashioneth** it with hammers, and worketh it with the strength of his arms: yea, he*

is hungry, and his strength faileth: he drinketh
no water, and is faint.

חָרַשׁ בַּרְזֶל מַעֲצָד וּפָעַל בַּפֶּחָם
וּבַמַּקָּבוֹת **יִצְּרֵהוּ** וַיִּפְעָלֵהוּ בִּזְרוֹעַ
כֹּחוֹ גַּם־רָעֵב וְאֵין כֹּחַ לֹא־שָׁתָה
מַיִם וַיִּיעָף

Isaiah 44:12

פלא (PLA) Strong's #6381-2/ AHLB #1380

A great action

Wonderous act

Freely vowing

Diverge from the norm

Separate

Sing unto him, sing psalms unto him: talk ye of
*all his **wondrous works**.*

שִׁירוּ־לוֹ זַמְּרוּ־לוֹ יֹחוּ בְּכָל־
נִפְלְאוֹתָיו

Psalm 105:2

Rest: Shabbat (שבת)

𐤕𐤐𐤔𐤔

__שבת__ (ShBTh) Strong's #7676 AHLB #2812

Day set aside for resting or celebration

Ceasing of work

7th day (Only day with a name)

Cease on going activity

Yah's day of rest

Cease

And he said unto them, This is that which Yahuah hath said, To morrow is the rest of the holy **sabbath** *unto Yahuah: bake that which ye will bake to day, and seethe that ye will seethe; and that which remaineth over lay up for you to be kept until the morning.*

וַיֹּאמֶר אֲלֵהֶם הוּא אֲשֶׁר דִּבֶּר יְהוָה שַׁבָּתוֹן **שַׁבַּת**־קֹדֶשׁ לַיהוָה מָחָר אֵת אֲשֶׁר־תֹּאפוּ אֵפוּ וְאֵת אֲשֶׁר־תְּבַשְּׁלוּ

בַּשֵּׁלוּ וְאֵת כָּל־הָעֹדֵף הַנִּיחוּ לָכֶם
לְמִשְׁמֶרֶת עַד־הַבֹּקֶר

Exodus 16:23

חדל (HhDL) Strong's #2308,2310/ AHLB #2148

Refrain from continuing an action

Refuse

Rejected

End

So Yahuah scattered them abroad from thence upon the face of all the earth: and they ***left off*** *to build the city.*

וַיָּפֶץ יְהוָה אֹתָם מִשָּׁם עַל־פְּנֵי
כָל־הָאָרֶץ **וַיַּחְדְּלוּ** לִבְנֹת הָעִיר

Genesis 11:8

השב (HShV) Strong's #2803-4,4284/ AHLB #2213

Resigning from plans

Joining

Thinking
Turning over thoughts
Design or purpose
Combining thoughts
Working
Skillfully

But as for you, ye thought evil against me; but Elohim meant it unto good, to bring to pass, as it is this day, to save much people alive.

וְאַתֶּ֞ם חֲשַׁבְתֶּ֧ם עָלַ֛י רָעָ֖ה אֱלֹהִים֙ חֲשָׁבָ֣הּ לְטֹבָ֔ה לְמַ֗עַן עֲשֹׂ֛ה כַּיּ֥וֹם הַזֶּ֖ה לְהַחֲיֹ֥ת עַם־רָֽב׃

Genesis 50:20

Special Thank You:

Amarayahu & Emunah
You are truly a Yah send. Thank you for showing me when my "hands" are building and even more importantly when they are destroying. It doesn't take a rocket scientist to spot foolishness, but it takes family to stand next to you with a hammer and nail to rebuild what has been destroyed.

To my "Girls":
I put that in parentheses because I dare not take away from the reverence and honor that your true position holds. Mom and Aunt Monae... I lack words for what it means to have family in this walk and even more so what it means to be privileged to have you as sisters in the faith. You two are the reason that I can do all that I do and also the ones who are my counselors and prayer warriors when I don't know how to move. You challenge me to walk circumspect to the Father as well as to be kind and humble in the face of adversity. I love you with all my heart!

Moreh Yoshiyahu Dauid
My teacher, My friend, and in this, my muse. We had a rough year lol! Yah has shown us how to walk together and how to agree. He has fused our purposes, but even greater he has solidified His reason for there being an "US". I thank you for remaining steadfast. I thank you for listening to all the lessons that came to my head for each chapter that have yet to be taught, and even more for standing on the truth at all times. You are it!

ABOUT THE AUTHOR

Huldah is of Malagasy Hebrew descent. It is the oral tradition of her family that they were taken from Madagascar on a Dutch slave ship to Holland. It was from Holland that her family made it to North Carolina. Huldah is a college graduate and an Educator. She currently lives in California. She is Married to the love of her life, and they have two beautiful daughters. Her passion and focus is the liberation of women and children through truth of their rich cultural heritage.

Notes

Notes

Notes

55995468R00142